STOICISM

Everything You Should Know To
Control Your Thinking, Build
Confidence, Train Your Mind and
Achieve True Happiness (Including Key
Principles And Practical Exercises)

By Charlie Holl

The content within this book has been derived from various sources. Please consult a licensed professional before attempting any techniques outlined in this book.

By reading this document, the reader agrees that under no circumstances is the author responsible for any losses, direct or indirect, that are incurred as a result of the use of the information contained within this document, including, but not limited to, errors, omissions, or inaccuracies.

Table of Contents

TABLE OF CONTENTSINTRODUCTION 4

INTRODUCTION 6

CHAPTER 1: WHAT IS STOICISM? 7
WHAT DOES STOICISM DO TO MANKIND? 8
FAMOUS FOLLOWERS OF STOICISM 15

CHAPTER 2: A BIT OF HISTORY 21
EPICTETUS 23
MARCUS AURELIUS... 24
SENECA 26

CHAPTER 3: STOIC PHILOSOPHY..28
PHYSICS AND LOGIC 30
IRRATIONAL PASSIONS... 32
GOOD PASSIONS 33

CHAPTER 4: KEY PRINCIPLES 34
STOIC VIRTUES.. 38

CHAPTER 5: THE STOIC LOGIC 43

CHAPTER 6: STOICISM AND HAPPINESS - THE STOIC TRIANGLE 49
STOICISM AND HAPPINESS.. 51
HOW HAPPINESS FEELS TO A STOIC... 58
HOW TO BE HAPPY BEING A STOIC USING THE STOIC TRIANGLE....................... 62

CHAPTER 7: MAIN BENEFITS 64
END SUFFERING 65
GRATITUDE 67
ACHIEVE SUCCESS... 69
CURE DEPRESSION 69
CHANGES YOUR MINDSET.. 71
YOU LEARN TO BE ALONE 73
LET GO OF YOUR EGO 75
GAIN CONTROL OVER YOUR LIFE 77
STOICISM HELPS IN BUSINESS 79

CHAPTER 8: OLD STOICISM VS MODERN STOICISM..........................**81**

STOICISM RULES TO FOLLOW IN THE MODERN ERA 85

CHAPTER 9: HOW TO PRACTICE STOICISM WITH PRACTICAL EXERCISES...........**88**

STOIC EXERCISES TO CHANGE YOUR LIFE 93
BONUS MEDITATION...130

CHAPTER 10: CORRELATION BETWEEN STOICISM AND BUDDHISM................**135**

CONCLUSION..**141**

BIBLIOGRAPHY **143**

Introduction

A philosophy that was created many years ago, stoicism is still incredibly helpful, even in the modern era. The stoic philosophy was derived to control emotions. A stoic person doesn't complain and can face hardships easily. Undoubtedly, stoicism can also be helpful in the endurance of pain.

Becoming a stoic can be difficult, but through this technique, you can master your thoughts. As the name of this book suggests, you can learn and master stoicism quite effectively.

How does one become a stoic? Well, this book is the answer to that question. This philosophy can make you stronger, and emotional turmoil will not affect you if you can learn how to behave as a stoic does.

The chapters of this book are filled with history, philosophy, and practical exercises to get a good grasp of stoicism at its best. I hope this book will be helpful and change your mindset to a great extent. I wish you all the best on the journey that begins now!

Chapter 1: What is Stoicism?

How often are you troubled with your own thoughts? That continuous tommyrot of crud running in your mind? These unnecessary thoughts of worry and negativity could be the reason for your grief or sorrow. Here's the good news: you can take control over your thinking via the amazing and practically methodical philosophy of stoicism. Stoicism is the popular antique Greek philosophy founded by Zeno of Citium in Athens while it was precariously in the third century BC. To be stoic is to be in the eye of a hurricane—to remain still and calm in the middle of whirlwinds of chaos and destruction. It's just not a philosophy, but a way of living which transforms the lives of many. There are some morals of stoicism, such as prudence, fortitude, justice, and moderation.

It has been practiced by many great people, one of whom was the Roman king Marcus Aurelius. The emperor was a paradoxical example of stoicism. Another famous historical person was Epictetus, and beyond him there are many more examples.

What Does Stoicism do to Mankind?

Stoicism gives us power over our thought process and allows us to become resilient enough to face the hardships of life. It can also save a soul from chaos. It is simply about endurance (mental, not necessarily physical) and our capability for patience as well as controlling negative emotions. There are many other things that happen to a stoic person such as a renewed admiration for reality, higher sense of justice, believing in themselves, and a better attitude towards life in general. Simply put, stoicism enlightens the mind and promotes better living through adopting self-control over devastating thoughts. It is the art of balancing human thoughts and emotions.

You can master your thoughts and improve your energy. Doesn't it seem fantastically empowering to get to know yourself better, control your thoughts in a way that benefits you, and find harmony in life? Stoicism embraces acceptance, and whether the outcome of any situation is good or bad it keeps you calm. It teaches you to accept reality.

According to science, the human mind is full of memories. But where does this memory come from? I'd say experience rather than thoughts. There can be certain experiences which create specific thoughts. For instance, a trauma during childhood may never be forgotten. This trauma can give your thoughts an everlasting impression. Thoughts are the fundamentals of human nature. You are what you think. Perception makes a huge difference.

According to the great Marcus Aurelius, "Very little is needed to make a happy life, it is all within yourself, in your way of thinking" (Marcus Aurelius, Hard, Marcus Aurelius & Fronto, 2011).

Let's understand this deeply. Thoughts are seeds which grow inside us. When you can grow a rose (good thought), then why should you grow weed (bad thought)? Every single day and every second of your life you are performing some kind of action. These could be physical, they could be mental, or emotional. In their entirety, these actions are very closely related to feelings, or you could say emotions. These thoughts make feelings, and feelings make emotions. Emotions in turn produce chemicals in our body and mind. In an easy language, you can call them "hormones."

Thoughts, feelings, emotions, and hormones give birth to some sort of energy within the body. It could be positive energy or negative energy. Stoicism shuts down negative thoughts and negative behaviors. It promotes a positive attitude towards life. It lets you see reality for what it really is and helps you with acceptance, too. Ultimately, stoicism changes one's mindset.

Epictetus was a Stoic philosopher of the 1st century AD, and together with Marcus Aurelius and Seneca he's known for being one of the big figures in Stoic philosophy. If you read more about him, you will find out that his teachings are actually quite enthralling.

Epictetus spent a portion of his life as a slave in the city of Hierapolis in Asia Minor. The fact that Epictetus was once a slave gives real credence and authority to his teachings. As you may know, stoicism is essentially about living as contentedly with life as you possibly can, no matter what the circumstances are. I can't help but feel that Epictetus' experience as a slave would have taught him a lot about acceptance and contentment. That really does shine through in his words.

He has penned down some of the best quotes and specific ideas for stoic teachers which I think are both relevant to us and also representative of stoicism as a whole. He said that everyone has to die, and he must have to as well. He explained his slavery by saying that his body was chained, but not his mind. Further, he added that no one could take his smile from him. I think these ideas are a good introduction into the central stoic concept: the idea that we are ultimately in control of our impressions and feelings. According to the Stoics, our will is our most precious possession as human beings.

Our will is our ability to make reasonable and sound judgments about our circumstances, and although our bodies might suffer or be imprisoned, our will never has to submit. Therefore, we can remain content even in the direst of circumstances. The only manacles that could ever truly entrap our minds are our own thoughts. Likewise, our mind has the power to undo all manacles which might be thrust upon us. We should all be familiar with the idea of acquiring contentment through the use of our will.

It's also worth considering the way that the Stoics view the world. The world can be divided into two broad categories, and this is a really easy equation. There are things which are out of our control—that is, all externalities and all circumstances outside of ourselves—and then there are things which are in our control and can all be reduced down to our will. The will is critically important, as we can use it to stop those externalities from disrupting our internal sense of contentment or equanimity. There are many quotes of Marcus' where he refers to luck and will. His words are so powerfully depicted that he used fortune in place of circumstances and faculty instead of will. Thus it's clear that our situations create our fortunes and our will can teach us a lesson or two.

The question is, why should we let circumstances override our will? The answer is to be happy. Now back to the word equanimity. It's a word often associated with stoicism and it typically is taken to mean composure, impartiality, or impassiveness. But there are more sources than just stony-faced acceptance. Stoicism is also brimming with a whole lot of gratitude. Gratitude for the fact that we are inhabiting this universe or at the scale a grandeur of this universe. So it's not right to dismiss this philosophy as being simply about tolerating bad things. Stoicism is a pair theistic philosophy, meaning that all things are viewed as being parts in a sacred whole. There's another quote which nicely illustrates that idea.

That quote says every human is connected to another. Man is also united with God, which is the supreme power of all. Basically, it says that we should be proud members of this divinely ordained universe.

But even so, we can't forget that stoicism is very concerned with obligations. It's not enough for us to live lives of perfect pleasure. The condition of us having pleasure necessitates that we are also exposed to all the pain that the universe might throw at us. We need to accept it all as part of the whole. We can't pick or choose what life throws at us. Everything is delivered in one incessant stream of totality. This requires us to have a broader perspective on our circumstances than we might be used to having. Epictetus gives us a great example when he asks us to consider that we have broken our leg and appreciate that this is far better than living without legs.

Because we're a part of this grand amazing universe, we need to accept what happens to us for the good of the whole. To get back to that theme of joy and gratitude, another concept is my favorite lesson at the moment. It reminds me that when I'm alone I don't need to consider it a wretched isolated condition. I don't need to feel that I'm missing out. Instead, I can see it as an opportunity for reflecting on the tranquility. Likewise, when I'm in a crowd, there's no reason to withdraw. Instead, I should take the opportunity to engage with my fellow humans to form connections and to interact. This is just really encouraging stoic advice.

Famous Followers of Stoicism

JK Rowling

The immensely successful best-selling author of the *Harry Potter* franchise is indeed a follower of stoic philosophy. She is a continuous follower of Marcus Aurelius, and he is one of her favorite philosophers. His quotes and meditations helped Rowling a lot in her difficult times. Keep in mind that before JK Rowling was a billionaire and a household name, she was just like anyone else. She went through 38 different rejections while taking care of her family as a single mother. Thus, she went through her fair share of adversities and she definitely used the stoic mindset of turning obstacles into the means to press forward. When many other people would have stopped and given up, she kept going. She's definitely a follower of the philosophy.

Neil Strauss

Author of *The Game*, Neil Strauss listed *On the Shortness of Life* by Seneca as one of his favorite books of all time. The interesting thing about this essay by Seneca is that it deals with the fact that we as humans think that life is short, when in reality our life is not short. We have ample time to do what we want. It's just that we waste a lot of our time on petty issues. We think about our neighbor's opinions, we waste time on things that are not going to be fulfilling, or on things that are not really going to matter in the future. Neil Strauss's story is very interesting, because he was selected as a writer for the New York Times Magazine. After some time, he became a pickup artist. He was kicked out of the magazine later. He got over that and became a best-selling author.

Lupe Fiasco

Grammy award-winning conscious rap artist Lupe Fiasco has been known to be an avid reader of Stoicism principles. In one of his songs "Lightwork," he dropped the following line; "Emperor is his alias, but not Marcus Aurelius." Lupe Fiasco has been known to recommend Marcus Aurelius's meditations. He has adapted many quotes and meditations of Marcus Aurelius in his life. Not only that, he even recommends reading and following stoicism and Marcus Aurelius's teachings to everyone. He's basically recommending that everybody absorb the stoic wisdom that has been laid out by the Emperor himself, Marcus Aurelius, so that we can all communicate on the same level and live better lives.

Nassim Nicholas Taleb

Another famous stoic is Nassim Nicholas Taleb, who is a Lebanese American essayist, a scholar aesthetician, as well as a former trader and risk analysis. He is well known for his best-selling book, *Anti Fragile*, in which he talks about the antifragility of stoic philosophy, especially Seneca's philosophy. According to him, a stoic is someone who can transform their insecurities or fear into prudence, pain into transformation, mistakes into initiation, and desires or wants into the undertaking. He basically just summarized the practical aspects of stoicism. Stoicism has the power to turn all the negatives in your life into something positive as well as turn every situation into a way for you to grow and become better. Stoicism is based on perception. Everything is about perception. So, we can determine the quality of our life by how we choose to perceive the events that happen. This is how famous philosophers have explained about how our life should be. So, a stoic is someone who sees the negative and chooses to transform it into good or into something that can help them.

Bill Clinton

The most famous person on this list is the former president of the United States, Bill Clinton. He was a big fan of Marcus Aurelius and his meditations. As a matter of fact, he said that he read the book once every year while he was president, which would make sense because Marcus Aurelius meditations were kind of like a personal diary for the emperor in which he wrote down notes on how he could live better, become nobler, and live a virtuous life in accordance with nature. Bill Clinton would have received a lot of value in reading these notes, especially because people don't change. Technology changes, but the human condition hasn't changed. We still face the same adversities in leadership and in life. Bill Clinton said that the thing about Marcus Aurelius is that he was deeply spiritual and he understood that life requires balance. His books also show what not to do as an emperor. He has mentioned what he wouldn't do, and that's really important. So clearly, Bill Clinton was heavily influenced by Marcus Aurelius.

All of these are the personalities who totally believe in living their lives to the fullest and not being stuck in any set role which is a part of it. A second is almost a fraction of our lives, and yet our lives are sufficiently long. As long as we can imagine. We need to make sure that we live our lives to the fullest.

Chapter 2: A Bit of History

To understand stoicism, it's helpful to learn a bit of history and how it emerged. It dates all the way back to 300 B.C.E. and was founded by Zeno of Citium, which today is Cyprus. It made its way to Rome, where it was embraced most notably by Marcus Aurelius.

Marcus Aurelius was a Roman Emperor and a powerful proponent of stoicism. He reigned both on his own and jointly for over 20 years, and during that time the Roman Empire benefited immensely from his wisdom and guidance. His own people as well as historians have commented on his sense of justice as well as his lifestyle of moderation. During his rule, the empire went through war, plague, and much suffering and hardship. Through it all, Marcus remained a stoic. He even penned one of the most famous philosophical writings, *Meditations*, which is more like a diary than a book on stoicism.

Stoicism is what is known as a "eudaimonic virtue ethic," which means that it proposes virtue as the main driver of happiness. It was intended to be a philosophy that could be applied to everyday life, and as such it only encouraged virtues that could be practiced consistently. That's one of the wonderful things about stoicism — it's incredibly practical.

There were three commonly identified phases of stoicism, the first of which began in 300 B.C.E. with Zeno. The second phase occurred during the time of Panaetius, and the last was during the Roman Empire. This last phase is the one most people are familiar with because it was the time of Marcus Aurelius, Epictetus, and Seneca. These were the three main proponents of stoicism, and it's really thanks to them that stoicism took off as much as it did and is so well known even today.

Each of these influencers practiced stoicism in their own way according to their life experiences. Epictetus was born a slave, Seneca was a wealthy senator, and Marcus Aurelius, as mentioned, was an emperor. Their life situations may have influenced to some degree their stoic practice, but the essence was the same for all, proving just how valuable stoicism can be for a wide range of people. We're going to look more in depth at the lives of each of these philosophers in order to understand where they drew inspiration from.

Epictetus

Epictetus began life as a slave, which is part of the reason why his stoic teachings are so beloved. While Marcus Aurelius and Seneca lived with riches, power, and freedom, part of Epictetus' life was spent in chains. Epictetus discovered philosophy when his owner let him pursue liberal arts studies. He first learned about stoicism from Musonius Rufus, then when he gained his freedom he decided to teach stoicism himself. For almost 25 years, this is exactly what he did.

Epictetus' teaching style was rather more strict than that of other stoics. He also used his time as a slave to develop his teachings and metaphors. He offered practical wisdom about how we can escape from our self-imposed chains and reach the freedom of soul that stoicism can provide. Much of his teachings are recorded in his book *Enchiridon*, which roughly translates to "handbook" or "manual."

Epictetus truly believed in mind over matter. He saw that many people of his time (and indeed in today's world) spent their lives seeking material gains, yet still could not attain happiness. He believed that the choice was between this way of living, and the way of a philosopher. He taught that mastery over your thoughts and mind brings greater wealth than money or possessions.

Some of his quotes that really highlight his way of teaching include:

"We have two ears and one mouth so that we can listen twice as much as we speak."

"He is a wise man who does not grieve for the things which he has not, but rejoices for those which he has."

"Nothing great is created suddenly, any more than a bunch of grapes or a fig. If you tell me that you desire a fig. I answer you that there must be time. Let it first blossom, then bear fruit, then ripen."

Marcus Aurelius

As has been mentioned, Marcus was a Roman Emperor, and one of the few classified as "one of the good ones." He is probably most noted for writing *Meditations*, which has come to be a core resource for modern stoics. Marcus' meditations are divided into 12 books, all of which follow closely to the teaching style of Epictetus. One main reason why *Meditations* is still so highly regarded is because Marcus details much of his inner thoughts and gives us a thorough introduction into how philosophy develops in the mind, in addition to how it can be applied to life.

As emperor, Marcus faced a unique set of challenges, temptations, and pleasures, all of which he was very careful to apply stoic teachings to. He placed heavy importance on his ability to control his desires and discipline his mind in every situation. He is perhaps the best example of how stoicism can help you in stressful times, because his entire life was spent under some amount of stress.

On of Marcus' teachers introduced him to the works of Epictetus, which was his first introduction into stoicism. In fact, in *Meditations*, the emperor goes so far as to thank his teacher for leading him to the stoic lifestyle.

Meditations contains many pearls of wisdom, notably three exercises that we can practice just as he did. The first exercise is practicing the virtues that we do possess rather than complaining or lamenting about those we don't, the second is looking to others for strength when needed (not being afraid to ask for help), and the third is maintaining a focus on the present. These exercises will be explored in a later chapter.

Some of Marcus' best quotes are below.

"When you arise in the morning, think of what a precious privilege it is to be alive - to breathe, to think, to enjoy, to love."

"You have power over your mind - not outside events. Realize this, and you will find strength."

"It is not death that a man should fear, but he should fear never beginning to live."

Seneca

Seneca was wealthy. Big time. At one point, he was even one of the wealthiest people in the Roman Empire. He serves as inspiration for many people today, including Tim Ferriss and Nassim Taleb, perhaps because he not only wrote about philosophy, he also spoke about how to use it.

Some have called Seneca a hypocrite, and it's not hard to see why. He was wealthy, powerful, tutor to Nero who would become one of history's most notorious leaders, and yet he wrote about morals and self-discipline. Seneca himself recognized this supposed hypocrisy, but he admitted that he was an imperfect man who was simply trying to make himself better.

If there is one stoic philosopher whose works you choose to read, make it Seneca. Not only are his works far easier to get through than others, they are full of wisdom that still applies in this day and age.

Similar to Marcus, Seneca proposed a few exercises to help those who read his works apply stoicism in their own lives. He advised finding a mentor, never letting your wealth control you or your actions, and rejecting ego at all costs.

Here are a few Seneca quotes to live by:

"Not how long, but how well you have lived is the main thing."

"A gem cannot be polished without friction, nor a man perfected without trials."

"Luck is a matter of preparation meeting opportunity."

Chapter 3: Stoic Philosophy

In its most literal definition of the word, stoicism is an ancient philosophy born in Greece and Rome. But when people hear the word philosophy, often they think it's not for them or that it's impractical. In reality, stoicism is the most practical philosophy ever made. Entrepreneur Tim Ferriss says that it's a personal operating system for the mind. Stoicism is a fantastic operating system for thriving in high-stress environments. I think that's the main reason that people like Marcus Aurelius adopted stoicism. Even entrepreneurs, artists, and athletes today are still using stoicism 2,000 years later for one main reason: it can help you solve your problems. In stoicism, there are three different disciplines. First of all, there is perception, or how you see things. Second of all, there's action - what you do about the things that you see. The third discipline is will, or how you bear and how you cope with the difficult things in life.

Stoicism, as mentioned, was founded in Athens by someone called Zeno of Citium. He was a merchant and in his life, he went through a horrible shipwreck. All of his belongings were taken away from him in his shipwreck. But through that process, he found philosophy and after him, there were three main famous stoics.

First, there was Marcus Aurelius, who was at the time the world's most powerful man, as he was the emperor of Rome and no man in the whole world was as powerful as him. Next was Epictetus, who was a slave and had an owner that would beat him. Then there was Seneca, who was a playwright. He was the most famous playwright in Rome, and he was also a political adviser. He was also one of the wealthiest men in the whole of Rome.

So you can see the diversity stoicism had, from absolute wealth, power, and riches to the complete opposite side of the spectrum—a slave who had nothing. It shows you that stoicism isn't like most philosophies, which are far removed from all of the inner workings of stoicism. It is a philosophy for the man or the woman in the workplace, the man or the woman competing in an athletic field, the philosophers, the politicians, the teachers, and everyone else in the world.

Stoicism is the philosophy for you, and it's the philosophy for me, because it acts as an inner compass that will help us make decisions day by day. It will help us have this sense of equanimity and a sense of being the best man or the best woman that we can be. Stoicism has a direct impact on every decision that we make and every decision that we think. It is being used to remove anxiety and depression and getting people to stop procrastinating, become disciplined, and start taking action. Stoicism is the best philosophy if you actually want to directly impact your brain and have it work in the most optimal way possible.

Physics and Logic

There are three main components of stoic philosophy, but the two most important will be discussed here briefly. The first is physics, which refers to the way the world works and all of its natural processes. The second is logic, which in essence is rational thought. The two aspects work in tandem to describe the way stoics view the world — through a lens of logic applied to reality.

Both physics and logic, even in the context of philosophy, can get a little complex, so only the basics will be covered here. Stoic physics gave stoics the ground to stand on, so to speak, by defining and exploring what the universe is made of and why it behaves the way it does. These explanations and observations could then be used to shed light on situations common to the human condition. Rather than life being one big enigma, stoics aimed to bring a little sense to the disorder.

Logic works with this by explaining the universe in ways that line up with reason. Stoic logic was extraordinarily similar to the logic that we know, teach, and use today, such as in computer programming. For example, if this, then this. Logics essentially explains what things are like and why they're not any other way by defining aspects of the world and statements as true and false.

The third aspect of the philosophy that we won't dive too deep into is ethics. Stoics through the ages have argued about where exactly ethics fits within the framework and what importance it holds, but the general view is that ethics cannot exist without logic, because logic can tell you what is ethical and what is not.

Irrational Passions

Irrational passions are what are known as voluntary responses, which as you can guess by the name are not positive aspects that stoics encourage. Irrational passions are also known as unhealthy or unnatural passions, indicating just how much the stoics felt they should be avoided. According to Zeno, unhappiness can be traced back to these irrational passions. There are many divisions and subdivisions of irrational passion, but what it all really boils down to is the following:

- Pain - envy, resentment, sorrow, anxiety, confusion

- Fear - shame, panic, shock, dread, superstition

- Craving - want, sexual desire, need for wealth and material possessions

- Pleasure - enchantment, spirited satisfaction

Stoics assert that these irrational passions lead to unhappiness. You might be uncertain as to why pleasure is on this list, but stoics believe that an excess of many things, including pleasure, is detrimental. Excess pleasure can cause us to forsake logic, which is a big no-no in stoicism.

Good Passions

Just as there are irrational passions, there is another side of the coin, the good passions. These are, you guessed it, the ones you want. These good passions aren't virtues, per se, but they contribute to our happiness and our ability to live virtuously. Keep in mind that the main thing separating the good passions from the irrational is that good passions stem from a place of reason. There is logic behind their existence, which makes them natural while the irrational passions are unnatural.

Good passions can be described as follows:

- Joy or delight (in place of pleasure)

- Caution or discretion (in place of fear)

- Wishing or willing (in place of craving)

All of these passions come from a place of logic and reason. Joy is a logical feeling stemming from something positive, caution is logical and necessary for self-preservation, and wishing is a natural human quality that is also logical, because wishing and/or willing is how to discover what's important to us.

Chapter 4: Key Principles

Stoicism works by bringing proper control over our thoughts. There are 10 key principles which are extremely essential in the life of a stoic.

1. **Work in harmony with nature to live your life** - As a normal person, it can be really difficult to differentiate between humanity and beast-like behavior. But stoicism explains this as a proper distinction. One should not behave like an animal, no matter what the situation is. Thus, you have to live a life that is full of agreement with life. There should be a reason for everything you do. This intellectual behavior of humans is what differentiates us from animals.

2. **Virtues** - Living a life which is full of virtues can be helpful to reach a higher level of humanity. There are four virtues to be followed by a stoic: wisdom, fairness or justice, fortitude or courage, and discipline in self. Through wisdom, one can have good sense and judgment. By implying justice, we can adapt fair behavior which imparts justice. Being courageous can induce a sense of confidence in you. Lastly, self-discipline teaches you to control yourself.

3. **Don't focus on what you can't change. Instead, focus on what can be changed by you** - No one should focus on what is not in their power. If someone is bothering you, it is not your fault. But, you can change your way of thinking and avoid such people. Don't let yourself suffer from the judgment of others. You have your thoughts and actions under control. Just focus on them.

4. **Good, the bad, and the undistinguished things** - Good things include virtues as explained earlier, and bad things are just opposite to these virtues. For example, cowardness, foolishness, stupidity, injustice, and indulgence are all examples of "bad." Next comes the indifferent things. These are the remaining parameters of life after bad and good things. Your wealth, health, and reputation are the indifferent things. These are called indifferent because stoicism suggests becoming indifferent towards these things. Your happiness does not depend upon whether you are healthy, rich, sick, or poor.

5. **Action** - Action is the biggest outcome of our life, and stoicism emphasizes on taking action quite literally. If you are on the way to become a stoic, then stop being lazy. Don't limit yourself based on the availability of

resources, time, or energy. Take action and turn your plan into reality.

6. **Get mentally prepared for the bad** - Stoicism explains that it is really practical to be aware of the forthcoming. You should be well prepared for misfortune. Get your sword and armor ready, no matter what happens to you. Stoics can change your mentality and prepare you beforehand. This method can also be termed as negative visualization. Don't fear the change, just be prepared for anything.

7. **Reserve Clause** - Do good by following your virtues, but be ready to accept the outcome. Your job is to just do good deeds, and the rest can be seen as the ultimate result. It can be in your favor or totally opposite to what you have expected. You have to act according to your virtues, but results are not under your control.

8. **Amor Fati** - You have to love everything that is happening around you. It may turn out to be good or extremely disastrous. Your thoughts and actions aren't to be affected by whatever is happening or has happened in the past. Love your fate and enjoy whatever happens.

9. **Your perception is your key** - Your obstacles can be your opportunities. What you perceive is what is. In

other words, perception can change your outlook over anything. Don't make judgments about anything. There is nothing that can make you happy or sad. It all depends on you.

10. **The greater the mindfulness, the greater the stoicism** - Be observant towards your thoughts and actions. Keep checking on yourself continuously. Be aware and be present in the current situation. Autopilot can be good, but sometimes it is merrier to take your life into your own hands.

Stoic Virtues

Stoic virtues were briefly mentioned above, but they're worth going into in depth. Wisdom, courage, temperance, and justice might all sound like old fashioned terms, but they're just as relevant today as they were in the times of ancient philosophers. You might be wondering what the point of virtues is and why they're talked about so often. At their core, virtues are like nirvana in Buddhism. They're the highest state that can be attained, and they display the greatest good that humanity is capable of. Stoics believe that every day, in every situation, an opportunity to call on one of the virtues presents itself. To start applying this ideal to your own life, you need to know exactly what the virtues are.

Wisdom

You've probably heard someone say it's important to know the difference between knowledge and wisdom. Stoics feel the same way. Knowledge is like book smarts. It's great to know a lot of things, but what do you do with all of that knowledge? That's where wisdom comes in. Information is of no use if you don't do anything with it, a fact which in and of itself is a piece of wisdom.

Wisdom guides action, which is one reason why it is so valued by stoics. Your actions and reactions are controlled by you and only you, and with wisdom you can learn which actions are right for which situations to take you further away from the irrational passions and closer to the good passions. Wisdom is, essentially, about applying the teachings of philosophy and stoicism. Without using wisdom, you'll know the facts, but not what they truly mean.

Temperance

Temperance is like the middle ground between too much and too little. It goes along with the concept of moderation, although it is far more fixed than moderation is.

Temperance is about knowing when enough is enough. This can apply to wealth, food, sexual desire, and the other "vices." Stoics recognize that while too much can lead to unhappiness, so can too little. Temperance is the guiding principle that allows you to still seek material gains while knowing when to stop.

It's not just applied to tangible items, of course. Temperance can also be applied to the irrational as well as good pleasures. Too much of a good pleasure can lead you towards irrational pleasures, and too much irrational pleasure leads to unhappiness. It's almost like a stoicism happiness scale that measures the goldilocks zone.

Temperance goes hand in hand with self-control. If you are able to control yourself in such a way that you don't sink too low or too high, you've found temperance and are well on your way to a stoic way of life.

Courage

Even if you feel like the cowardly lion, there is courage buried within you. We don't often have to reach for courage in our modern society, so when we do it can be hard to find. Stoicism is the perfect way to flex your courage muscles, so to speak. Courage isn't just about rushing into battle or facing down a foe. It's about conquering fear of the little things, too.

Maybe you're afraid to get a new job. Or start a hobby. Or join a gym. Or countless other things that permeate our modern society and have become the new battlefields. Life is full of small fears and seemingly insignificant barriers than, no matter how small, hinder us nevertheless. Through stoicism, you can find the courage you need for every situation, big or small.

Marcus Aurelius was courageous not just because he went to war, but also because he resisted temptation and refused to let power corrupt him, despite how easy it would have been to give in. Seneca's death was ordered by Nero, his pupil, yet he faced death with the words, "Nero can kill me, but he cannot harm me."

You won't always win. Not every battle is going to end in victory. But that's the other side of courage: continuing to push forward and fight, even when you know it's hopeless. It takes real courage to live a real life. Stoicism can give it to you.

Justice

You're probably thinking of popular judge shows right now, and you're not too far off. But stoic justice is more about a personal practice than a community oriented sense.

In order to understand justice, it's easier to think of what injustice is. Something that is unjust inflicts harm on another being. There is no cavet stating whether or not the person deserved it. Harm or injury to another, physically or otherwise, is simply unjust. Plain and simple.

To act with justice is to act with more than your own interests in mind. This isn't selflessness, per se, but it does involve a wider view than the self-centered nature most of us are used to inhabiting. It's easy to understand why we are this way. We all live within our own heads and are consumed by our own lives. However, we can learn to widen our view and take others into consideration.

You might consider justice to be a duty to your fellow humans, and a duty they have to you. Equality, fairness, respect—these are all aspects of justice. Justice is also the foundation of the other virtues. What is courage without justice? What is wisdom? How can you have temperance if you don't also incorporate fairness and respect? Justice is the holy grail, and if you strive towards any virtue, make it this one.

Chapter 5: The Stoic Logic

Stoicism is a philosophy that I've been living and practicing for quite some time. It is really important to know about how Stoics react to specific unfortunate and uncomfortable events. This could be the death of a family member, losing your job, getting dumped by your partner, or even something as tiny as going grocery shopping while you're angry. I want to clarify what stoicism actually is. Stoicism follows the belief that practicing specific virtues, such as wisdom, results in long-term happiness. Furthermore, stoicism is a very practical philosophy because it is based on the belief that we cannot control external events or our circumstances. Yet stoics have the power to react to these events in a specific manner. Stoics are able to objectively react and cope with the struggles of life. They pursue objectivity and logical reasoning instead of impulsiveness and giving in to our inner urges.

Stoicism is about accepting that we are on this planet for a short duration. We have to realize that not only we ourselves are short-lived, but also everything that we experience in our lifetime. In my opinion, stoicism is one of the best if not the best approach to getting more out of life. It is rational, and it is especially beneficial for people who strive for improvement, as it focuses on controlling immediate urges like food cravings or addiction. It is therefore not only beneficial for our careers, but also for our health.

Unfortunate life events, as already mentioned, could be losing a loved one, losing your job, losing your house, not getting a job, failing an exam, or pretty much anything that seems really really unpleasant. Most people will be either pissed off or sink into a deep hole of self-pity. For example, we could be mad because our boss is not realizing how qualified we actually are. We could be angry because our teacher did not tell us about all the material that was required for the class. We could sink into self-pity because our girlfriend broke up with us. Lastly, we could even sink into a deep depression because we lost a sibling, a parent, or another much-appreciated person.

Whatever it may be, all of these reactions are by no means stoic. Instead, these are quite the opposite. They are an emotional, uncontrolled, and impulsive reaction to circumstances. A better explanation is this - it is simply not in our hands, or it is neither changing the situation in itself nor making us happier or benefiting us. I'm not saying we shouldn't feel grieved because we've lost someone. That's probably not possible for most people. Yet, we can control ourselves at least.

Imagine one of your friends going through one of these struggles. Either he lost someone, or he didn't get a job, or he didn't pass his exam. What would be your advice, or what would you tell him to do instead of increasing his negative feelings? Would you say yes, you deserved to fail that exam? You would probably encourage them, tell them we learn through our failures, it's just an exam, you can retake it easily, and next time you'll be prepared and then you're going to ace it. Or if he just got dumped by his girlfriend, you would probably not mention how ugly he is. Neither would you say that he's a jerk and he should have paid more attention to his relationship.

Instead, you would probably suggest that he move on. After all, they are plenty of fish in the sea. It is only one woman that dumped him, and there are so many more out there. Plus, she didn't deserve him in the first place. You might finish up with a phrase like, "That's just how life is. Nothing lasts forever."

We can clearly understand both sides, as we understand impulsive behavior, grief, and sadness, but we also understand the motivating side. So, the shift we want to make is to go from sadness and grief to the more objective and motivating view. We are in an unfortunate situation, but instead of impulsively reacting, we take a step back. We take an objective view. We give ourselves the same advice and we act in the exact same way that we would suggest someone else act. This can be quite hard, because we are frequently overruled by our emotions. Nevertheless, it is possible to remain objective, reasonable, and logical.

As a result, we will be able to control our own emotions better than our own reactions. We just need to reflect on the situation and understand that our reaction is our own doing. And yes, this is way easier said than done. Try reflecting on your situation. If you just got dumped, it's insanely hard to be a good friend to yourself, and following the advice given earlier is by no means easy. Yet if we practice this approach for all negative events, then we will eventually get better at it. After tediously working on controlling our emotions, we will eventually remain more rational when an unfortunate event strikes us. By being objective, we will not only minimize the feelings of sadness, anger, and hate, we also make the right decisions.

We won't be shouting at our spouse because we lost our job or we won't be losing our job because we fell into a deep depression after our mom died. We managed to keep it all under control. These gigantic events are fairly rare, and practicing them is beneficial but not really easy. Therefore, we have to practice self-control in our everyday life. We face hundreds of decisions each day, and we can train our self-control by not giving in to the bad decisions. We increase our strength by not giving in to our urges. We buy a salad instead of steak. We exercise instead of popping in another movie. We get up early instead of sleeping in.

In a nutshell, stoicism is a practical approach to living a better life. Stoics believed that they cannot control all of their circumstances, but they can control their reaction. Being rational is a quintessential part of stoicism, and this means that we should practice self-control, resist our immediate urges, and fight impulsive behavior, as these will only bring us into a downward spiral.

Chapter 6: Stoicism and Happiness - The Stoic Triangle

Do you realize that at the end of the day, we really only have control over one thing? We don't have control over the weather, over the actions of other people, or on our genetics, nor over our past. None of that! But we can control our minds. We can't control the external, but we can control our thoughts and with our thoughts, we can influence our emotions and control our actions. Even that alone can be extremely powerful. The key here with stoicism is to keep in mind that there is the only thing that we can control. Most people go through similar kind of things their entire lives and they go around thinking or not even thinking. They just kind of go around through their daily lives as if they have control over everything or rather worrying about everything external. They worry about the opinions of others, they worry about what the weather is going to be like, they worry about this or that, or they blame their genetics or their past or where they were born.

But the thing is, stoics realize that the only thing that we really can control is our minds. With that realization, the only thing that's really worth even focusing on or putting our time and energy into is optimizing our thoughts and having a high-quality mindset. That will lead to a life and a lifestyle that can breed peace of mind, happiness, and confidence. We have to keep in mind that what we need to do on a daily routine is to realize that. We shouldn't focus on or worry about anything outside of our control. So the next time something happens to you that's outside of your control, whether it's the weather, bad luck, or whatever it is, just keep in mind that the thing was bound to happen.

How you react to the situation really defines your character, and really will end up boiling down to more confidence for you. So if you do get into a car crash, or if something bad happens to you, remember how you have to respond to the situation. If you stay cool, calm, and calculated in that situation and you don't really stress about it, you don't really worry, and you still focus on the other good things that are going to come to you throughout your day, then afterward you know it's going to actually be easier for you to continue to focus on your thoughts and on your mind.

Stoicism and Happiness

Through stoicism, you are going to learn the exact method to raise your default level of happiness. I'm not talking about happiness from external objects like money or fame or anything like that. I'm talking about increasing your level of joy so you have this deep-rooted fulfillment that gives you pleasure at every moment of life, regardless of what your external circumstances are. Let us start with a quote from Seneca, who was a great philosopher back 2,000 years ago. According to him, true happiness is all about enjoying the present moment.

Someone who is not anxious about the future is also happier on the inside. Seneca said that someone who can be satisfied with what he already has is the real human. A human who has every contentment inside him. True happiness can be experienced by avoiding being anxious and without depending on the future. Seneca has told us so many things about being happy.

But don't get confused and think that Seneca is telling us that we shouldn't better ourselves or shouldn't aspire to gain material possessions in this world. This isn't the case, because Seneca himself was a very wealthy man. What he is telling us is actually an admonition against the lack of presence. People tend to forget about the present moment. We're always looking into the future and we're always looking into the past. We're always wishing for things, trying to get the next best thing and are never content with our lot. We suffer from the monkey mind, the distracted mind that lacks focus.

Of course, this is part of the human condition, and this is part of the social narrative. We are always thinking ahead, thinking of the family, our jobs, something we want to buy, or retirement. But the trap is that we miss out on living. We miss out on the present moment. Happiness is now. I really don't want you to get confused by this quote, thinking that Seneca is advising us not to want external things like money or happiness from external objects. If Seneca won the lottery, of course, he'd accept it. Seneca was a very wealthy man, so naturally he wouldn't advocate for less.

That's not the point. Instead, the point is to be content with what you have before you start looking for external things. To increase your happiness, Seneca is advising us to be completely present in the moment, stop thinking about the past, and stop thinking about the future. Neither of those things is real, because in the future that moment in time will be the present moment. You can't change the past, for it's done, and you can't change the future because it hasn't happened yet. All you have is the present moment, so live now in this present moment. Get into the present moment, and be aware of your surroundings.

Be aware that you're sitting down. Feel the scene, whether you are sitting on the bed or a couch or a chair. Sit and just be in the present moment. Take this time now to enjoy what you have. Stop thinking about the past, stop worrying about the future, and just be present right now. Whilst reading this book, appreciate that you have this time alone and that you have your computer or phone or wherever screen you're using. Just be completely present.

What happens over time is, our monkey mind gets completely distracted. It's only within our brain that we get an increase in happiness from external objects. Say, for example, you win the lottery and after some time your happiness increases a little bit. But after a week or a month or a year, your happiness goes back down to the default level. This is called the hedonic treadmill in science, and it states that whenever an external event happens to you, your happiness changes for a little bit. Whether it be a positive change or a negative change, after time you return to the default level of happiness.

This is just human nature, and this is what happens. This is why so many lottery winners enjoy the money for a certain length of time. After a while, their expectations increase, which brings the default level of happiness back down to where they were before they won the lottery. It's exactly the same thing if something negative happens. Say something is stolen from you. For a while you're annoyed at yourself, thinking why did I let this happen? But then, as time goes on, you return to your default level of happiness.

The advice that Seneca is giving you is to increase that level of happiness. To stop fluctuating between happiness and negative raises the bar completely. So, you can be completely content and completely joyful at all times. Let's reflect back. Think of when you were younger and you wanted something, like a toy. Now, let's say this thing you wanted it was an Xbox One, the first Xbox. When you were younger, you probably thought that this thing would bring you lots of happiness. You had dreams about it, you talked about it, and you begged your parents to buy it for you. If you were lucky, perhaps your parents did give in and they bought you the Xbox.

For the first few weeks or so, you were ecstatic. You were very happy, and you had heaps of joy as you played this thing. You played it until the gimmick wore off. What naturally happened is you started growing tired of it, so the happiness faded and you wanted something more. You wanted something else to rekindle that excitement. So the next thing you go for is maybe the Xbox 360, or a new bike, or maybe a new laptop, and so begins the cycle. Let me tell you a quick story that will help you internalize this point.

A few years ago, I wanted a new laptop. I dreamt about. I was obsessed with the idea, and I saved money from time to time, convincing myself that when I got this laptop I would be happy. I'd be completely content. So I got the laptop, and I was right! I was happy and I was completely content for a week, maybe. Then after a week, I got bored of the laptop and I wanted something better. This is the hedonic treadmill. My happiness level increased, but then it went back to the default level of happiness.

Now, this cycle doesn't end during childhood. It continues to adulthood. We are always looking for new job positions, new cars, new material things, new positions, or all of the above. But at the end of the day, we end up going back to a base level of happiness. Why are we never able to truly be content or fulfilled? Because there is always something else. It never ends.

If you were to lose your house right now and start living on the streets, of course you might be depressed to begin with. You might actually be suicidal for a while, but after a few months, maybe a year or two, your base level of happiness goes back to where it was. You adapt to the situation.

If you were to become a multimillionaire right now, you'd be pretty happy and you'd have a lot of time to enjoy yourself, but after a few years, once again, your base level of happiness returns to its normal level. This is why people are so surprised when they see celebrities that get depressed or commit suicide. This is what people don't understand about the hedonic adaptation. Material things don't matter.

After a while, things change, but happiness comes from within and it comes from paying attention to the present moment and enjoying it without really needing anything more. Once again, this doesn't necessarily mean that you shouldn't aspire for great things, but it means that you should be able to take some time to reflect, sit down, and enjoy the present moment.

Think of ways that this has happened in your life, and I promise you will find some resemblance to this situation. Then, remind yourself that you can stop looking for external things to increase your level of happiness, because happiness comes from within. I urge you to understand that happiness resides within yourself. You have happiness inside of your body. Just realize that, and you will be joyful, I promise.

How Happiness Feels To A Stoic

I'm going to guess that you've already read multiple articles and have gone through multiple books about happiness, and yet your happiness hasn't multiplied. Why is that? Listening and reading aren't the same as doing. All behavior, and all changes, must be trained. Stoics didn't write their material solely to be read. They created practical exercises in order to train your mind to respond properly to life so that you could live it well. Stoicism isn't concerned with difficult sayings and philosophies. Its focus is on helping us overcome harmful feelings and work on the things that can be changed.

Simply put, here are the Stoics most important exercises for happiness:

Get Rid of Your Obstacles

This exercise is very powerful, because if you can properly fight your obstacles and get rid of them, you can become happy. Every bad becomes a potential source of good to the stoic. Everything is an opportunity. For example, situations where your hard work is underpaid or the demise or loss of a loved one occurs are not considered opportunities, generally. In fact, they can make you weak because they are obstacles. What do the stoic do? They believe there is a lesson to be learned in each and every experience we have in life, and that every obstacle that comes our way leads to more growth.

Rather than sulking or complaining, stoics ask themselves, "What have I learned from this experience?" and "How have I become a better person?" These are empowering questions. Most of us are not completely immune to external events or the bad things that happen to us. These result in bad feelings within us. However, recognizing that our lives still go on and we can't pity our situations is an outlook that can give us a completely different way of living. More importantly, this outlook can make us strong in adverse situations.

Is This Within My Control?

One of the most important practices in stoic philosophy is differentiating between what we can change and what we can't. Let's say a flight was delayed because of the weather, and no amount of arguing with the airline representative will end the bad weather. In another example, physically we may be taller or shorter than we want, but no amount of wishing will change that. What's important to realize is the time spent mulling over these unchangeable situations is often wasted. Don't fight the battles you can't win. When you realize that you can't control certain things, you feel happier.

Appreciate the Present

Chasing future happiness is self-defeating. We can find happiness by accepting the present. If you refuse to accept your reality and always hope that you deserve a better future, this can result in robbing yourselves and present happiness. By seeing happiness as an outcome of some future achievements such as getting a certain job, more money, or finding a spouse, we start to lose sight of what we already have as our happiness right in this very moment. And even worse the plans for the future happiness do not go as desired. We will grow depressed similar to chasing future happiness. The Stoics believe that developing a constant desire for one thing after another can be a reason to unhappiness. So they implanted the idea of accepting and gratifying things that are already there. By doing so, you can find ultimate satisfaction in whatever you have.

How to be Happy Being a Stoic Using the Stoic Triangle

Eudaimonia

The main mantra of stoicism is eudaimonia. This phenomenon explains how to be happy with your higher self or how to stay calm on the inside. In other words, this part of the happiness triangle can also be explained by supreme happiness. How to achieve this? Just be good to your inner domain and follow three famous principles of stoic happiness triangle, which are explained as follows:

1. Live with Areté - To do this, you have to align your innermost beliefs (good ones) with your actions. Just become the best version of yourself and express yourself a lot.

2. Focus on the controllable things - The most prominent teaching of stoicism is to focus on what you can control rather than what is not in your control. Accept whatever is happening around you, whether it is good or bad, but have control over your actions and your thoughts.

3. Be responsible - Take responsibility for your life. External events can't make you happy or miserable. It's solely up to you how to react in different situations. If you can become responsible about how you choose to stay calm despite the external happenings, you are on your way to being extremely happy.

Chapter 7: Main Benefits

Stoicism found its way into my life a few years ago, and I found it to be the most useful and practical philosophy I have ever read. It's actually remarkable that anything from 2,000 years ago can shine a light on modern problems of existence, but it really does. I've broken down my ongoing journey into stoicism into a number of useful and easily conceptualized insights. Each of these benefits is what people around the world have experienced. The best method to live a happy life is to have some problems to deal with. As we deal with them, we should make a game of the hardships. Each hardship is an opportunity to conquer the enemy within ourselves. We have no control over many of life's tragedies entering our world, but we can control how heroically we choose to act when they arrive.

When hardships arrive, think *Wow, I get to see if I can deal with this!* Cultivate the same mindset as a sportsman would have when trying to achieve something. Turn it into a game or objective. Lifting weights in the gym is an opportunity to grow your muscles, and meditating is an opportunity to become calm. A tragedy is a wondrous training ground for heroism, as such a tragedy is a blessing. When one's focus is on the game of cultivating heroism and not on the unfairness of existence, then tragedy becomes opportunity, and opportunity is fun.

End Suffering

You might take this thinking even further. Let's say that suffering can at least be partially prevented by learning to act well in the world. Let's say that we can learn to act well through suffering, that suffering itself teaches us the wisdom to remove suffering. We might then desire to encounter as many challenging and chaotic situations as possible in order to learn how to prevent them. I'm heartened by this concept, as it has that paradoxical nature which those deep universal truths seem to have.

Negative visualization is one of those trademark stoic techniques. You think of losing the things you hold most dear in your life. If you're doing this technique well, you will picture these horrible things very vividly. To my understanding, there are some huge benefits from pressing this technique. The first is that you are inoculated when those monstrous things never actually happen. You become prepared emotionally, and it also encourages you to make some physical preparations. Second, if something actually does happen, you were already mentally prepared for it, so the shock is less severe.

Gratitude

Another benefit is that you appreciate what you already have. It's hard to take what you have for granted when you consider losing it. Here's an example: everyone is used to using their legs. What would it be like to lose them? Your ability to walk would be severely affected. You're probably taking your ability to walk today for granted. But if you pause for a moment and reflect on the real possibility of losing this gift, then you'll feel gratitude. Holding the feeling of gratitude is good, and having more gratitude for the things we already have is even better. It is an antidote to the outer problem of always needing more.

Comforting doesn't work in the slightest and actually makes anxiety worse. Instead, the solution lies in cultivating a robust mindset. This can be achieved by practicing dealing with challenging situations.

I also find that stoicism is a magnificent tool for cultivating the mindset necessary to become wealthy and appreciate that wealth. Part of its brilliance lies in teaching us not to require wealth to make us content. Freedom from the need and desire for wealth is empowering, and it allows us to freely receive it without attaching to it. It also gets rid of the vices associated with wealth that can turn it from a positive into a negative.

One such vice is the need for wealth that overrides all else to the point where important things in your life become overlooked. Do you need to dress in fancy clothes to feel okay, do you need an expensive haircut, do you need a flashy car? If you need these luxuries to maintain your internal tranquility, then the luxuries control you, and I would add that this makes you weak. So from time to time, free yourself from your internal tyranny by learning how to not require the luxuries that wealth brings.

The Roman stoic Cato famously dressed in a cheap toga. Fancy or expensive clothing was just of no use to him. See adversities as an opportunity to learn the virtue of making or being resilient. Follow this thinking through, and you may even find yourself becoming excited about making do with the humble things in life, just as the marathon runner might be excited by a long road or the mechanic by looking at a broken-down engine. The challenge of poverty itself becomes joyous.

Achieve Success

When you are less concerned about others, you become more focused on your own success. Protect your time. This is the number one rule of history—to focus on this single theme. Successful people don't let anyone waste their time. A stoic can easily say no to anyone. This makes you even more successful at your workplace. Founders of stoicism could never fully express their bafflement at the darkness of the human mind. When other people and events try to steal time from you or your work, remind yourself of what the founder of IKEA has observed. You can do so much in 10 minutes time.

Cure Depression

Let me start this section off with a disclaimer: if you are severely depressed and suicidal, seek help immediately. Stoicism can help depression in ways that will be explained shortly, but it should not be used as a replacement for therapy and proper treatment if you need it. Do not be afraid to look for guidance from an outside source.

Even the great Emperor Marcus was sometimes unable to get out of bed. Even he on occasion felt that deep need to hide from the world and retreat into a place of safety and security. We all have days when we would rather not face what's out there. But this isn't healthy, and it's not how our lives are supposed to be lived. Stoicism can help.

Depression is often a result of our outlook and expectations. We want something specific from the world that we won't always witness or receive, and that disappointment can manifest as depression when we realize there's very little in the world under our control. It's not easy to get out of bed when you look at the world and don't like what you see, but if you reframe your mindset and see in a different way, you might just be able to drag yourself up.

Stoicism reminds us to face the world, no matter what comes, and to keep our expectations in line with reality. Look at the world through realistic lenses and see it for what it really is. Reframe depression. Instead of seeing a bleak world full of bad people and sadness, see humans that are all like you, all trying to figure out their place, and appreciate the fact that you can even contemplate your existence. Change the way you look at the world, and the world will change.

Additionally, since stoicism is more about logic than emotion, it can help you pin down the feelings of depression and get to the root of the problem. Often, when we are depressed, we also feel a sense of helplessness because we don't always know what's causing the depression or how to stop it. When you focus less on the emotional aspect and more on the logical, you're better able to identify exactly what is underlying your blues and can take steps to overcome whatever it is that's the problem.

Changes Your Mindset

Stoicism helps you to recognize that most things are external. It helps you let go of all ill thoughts that come from a misinterpretation of reality. When you think about it, that's a very interesting idea. You're misinterpreting reality, and that's why you're not happy. When you're upset and you have these ill thoughts, it's because you are thinking that there's some kind of maliciousness about the world and reality, and you're not accepting it. So, all of those ill thoughts that you have come from a misinterpretation.

The world is not against you. In fact, you can view other people the same way, because they're part of the world and they're part of reality. If someone is mean to you or they treat you poorly or they do the wrong thing to you, you can treat them objectively. You can say, "This is not bad and this is not good, this is what has happened and I can choose how I want to deal with it." It doesn't mean that you're never going to feel pain or have emotions. A lot of people confuse stoic philosophy with not having emotions, or being indifferent to pain and pleasure. In reality, it means that you are indifferent to pain or pleasure and regardless of the feeling of pain or pleasure which you do feel, you continue to take the same actions as you would if there were no pain or pleasure.

You have in your mind what you want to do, who you want to become, and what actions you want to take, and you do not get swayed by pain, fear, or any other emotion. Instead, you keep on going forward towards your goal.

You Learn to be Alone

I like the idea of abstracting yourself from everything external. Stoicism says that this is life, so accept it the way it is or you will suffer again. You will suffer if you're not willing to accept what is happening or what reality is. How this girl or guy has treated you, what you look like, what your financial situation is...whatever it is, if you cannot accept reality, then you are going to suffer. As soon as you accept reality, and as soon as you accept that this is what has happened, you can go through it quite easily. You have to accept things to move on.

How this relates to being alone is that you realize another person's perception of you is their problem, and your perception of yourself is your problem. You need to care a lot more about what you think of yourself than what anyone else does. What you honestly think about yourself is not about the image that you're trying to portray. Do you really think that you've worked hard enough, that you're maximizing your potential, or that you're living your life full of excellence? Or are you just putting on a show so that the whole world can give you praise? You might seem like you have it all together, but if you feel like you're a fraud, if you know that you haven't done what you need to do with your life and if you're not pleased with yourself, it doesn't matter.

That's how stoicism changes your mindset. It makes you strong enough to face the world and its problems. You realize you are alone even when there are people around you. There is no one else but you inside your head unless you let other people be inside your head. This allows you the unique opportunity to really know yourself, without the noise of others drowning out your own inner voice. Often, we think through the filter of the opinions of others. We let people take up space in our heads not because we want them there, but because we don't decide not to. We hear judgements, criticisms, and reprimands, none of which come from our own conscience. Our minds are accompanied by what we think everyone else thinks instead of what we feel. How often do you focus on shutting out every other thought but your own? Stoicism can help you with this. It can help you tune out every other voice so that you alone are the one occupying space in your mind, and that aloneness is a gift. By banishing outside influences, you free your mind and regain control. Your own mind is the only one that can speak your truth.

Let Go of Your Ego

Ah, ego. We all have it. Some of us have too much of it. Ego refers to your self-esteem and sense of personal importance, both of which are fundamental human concepts. Self-esteem is vital, particularly if you hope to accomplish anything in your life. Nothing in stoicism says you have to sacrifice self-esteem for a lack of ego, so don't think that's what this section is about.

Instead, what stoicism teaches is that too much ego is detrimental and is a factor that leads to unhappiness. This idea shouldn't be too surprising. After all, how often have you heard of a "bruised ego," or thought of someone as "egotistical"? Neither of these are very positive, indicating that ego isn't always a good thing.

Think about the last time someone critiqued your work. If the critique wasn't 100% positive or in your favor, you may have felt a little hurt. Annoyed, even. Maybe you discounted what they said because you didn't agree with it. All of these reactions trace back to one thing: ego. These reactions come from a feeling of lack, as if our personal worth has been questioned and attacked when of course it hasn't been. That's what ego does, though. It makes everything personal. That leads to unhappiness, and unhappiness is something stoicism knows how to deal with very well.

Stoicism can teach you that it really isn't about you after all. Your reaction is what turned the situation from a neutral event into a personal attack. If you can reframe your mindset and alter your reaction, you eliminate the issues ego causes.

Let's take an example. Suppose you've just submitted a report to a higher up detailing the financial state of your department. You put a lot of work into this report, so naturally your ego is involved. You have tied your worth and importance into it, so its reception will be a direct reflection on you as a person. At least, that's what ego says. If the higher up has a problem with it, you'll see it as a problem with you, not the report itself, and you will either feel bad about yourself or be unhappy with the higher up. Both of these are reactions that you have control over. If you choose the third option, to look at the situation as a neutral party with no personal interest in the matter, you can see beyond the emotional ego side of it and look at the logic. Not only does this promote an internal peace, it also helps you become a better person and employee.

Gain Control over Your Life

This might seem paradoxical since we have been discussing the lack of control you have over most of your life, but there really is some truth to this. When you recognize what you can't control, you begin to see what you can. Once you see there are areas of life you can influence, you begin to take more of an interest in managing those areas.

People tend to have two attitudes towards life. The first is to try desperately to control everything, then become frustrated and unhappy when the things that are obviously out of your control don't go the way you wanted them to. The second is to assume that since some things are out of your control, there is nothing that is in your control so you can float through life and let whatever happens happen. Neither of these are encouraged by stoicism, and neither will lead you to a happy life.

True stoicism is somewhere in between these two attitudes. On one hand, it encourages an acceptance that some things are out of your control, and those should be left alone to play out without any attempted interference on your part. On the other, it also asks that you recognize and embrace what you can control. Go with the flow, until you can alter it in some way.

When you become a stoic, you can more easily navigate through your life. You can control what you are saying, what you are doing, and what you are thinking. This pretty much makes it hassle-free to react and respond in some situations where non-stoics struggle.

Stoicism Helps in Business

The life of an entrepreneur is tough, but stoicism can help. After all, it teaches three core principles that can aid you personally and professionally. These principles include the fact that the world is unpredictable, you have control over yourself, and dissatisfaction comes from a lack of logic when regarding circumstances. Let's look at how each of these apply to entrepreneurs and the business world.

Firstly, the world is unpredictable. This we know. But in business, especially when the stakes are high, we tend to forget this until something happens, then we react poorly. Stoicism pushes this fact into our face and doesn't let us forget it. Life isn't predictable. It's not supposed to be. What would be the fun in knowing exactly what's going to happen at all times? Sure, you wouldn't encounter nasty surprises, but there would be no good surprises either. That kind of life isn't worth living. So, be glad that you can't predict what's going to happen next. Revel in the mystery. And, in business, remember that even if you plan everything out, something could still change your plans. Don't pull an attitude and curse the world. Instead, pivot. Readjust. Move with the changes. You never know what's going to happen next.

Second, you control you. You don't control investors, your business partner, your family, or your customers. Accept that, like the world, they can be unpredictable. That's a good thing. It's part of the human condition. So refrain from gripping onto anyone in your business and professional circle and attempting to exert your influence forcefully. It won't do you any good and could in fact hurt your chances of business success. No matter what those around you do, you can't control it, so control how you react instead.

Third, a lack of logic applied to situations is what makes them seem ugly or negative. Emotions are part of life, but they can be detrimental in business situations. When you react to situations that revolve around partnerships, customers, finances, or other business aspects in a negative and emotional way, problems quickly follow. Train yourself to approach your business with pure logic. Whatever happens should be considered and evaluated before a decision based on observation, not emotion, is made.

Chapter 8: Old Stoicism vs Modern Stoicism

Since we are human, we try to control as many things as possible to free ourselves from feelings of vulnerability and confusion to ultimately find happiness. To be able to deal with such situations, you can look to stoicism. Stoicism is an ancient philosophy which can be a great help with controlling thoughts.

Early stoicism was just based on how you can control yourself. It worked for some of the greatest emperors and kings. You can even argue that its ideas are more important than ever in this day and age because of social media. It is an aid in the popular movement of self-improvement. Writers like Tim Ferris and Robert Greene have written about stoicism and increased its popularity. People look to follow the teachings of stoicism to find calmness, peace within, and to better deal with all the chaos around them.

To better understand stoicism, we will look at the life and writings of Marcus Aurelius. Marcus Aurelius was a Roman emperor who had absolute power. He had a powerful army that was feared, he could have any woman he wanted, and he could have chosen to just have fun for the rest of his life. Momentary pleasure was available to him without limits.

But unlike some people who are corrupted by power, Marcus was different. He wrote about his struggles within himself in the now famous *Meditations*. Stoics observed that there are things not in our control, and most of these things are outside our mind. On the other side of this, there are things in our control, which are our internal thoughts, interpretations, and reactions. Reality does not care about our opinions, nor can we will it to, but it doesn't mean we are helpless victims of the world.

Most things are simply not up to us, like the attitudes of our colleagues or how the economy is doing, and there is nothing we can do to exclude misfortune. What is under our control are our opinions, actions, and how we interpret the world around us. Stoics focus on the things they can control. When we believe that things outside ourselves or things in the future will bring us happiness, we become dependant on things outside our control, which is not ideal to a stoic. This doesn't mean we live an inactive life, but this means that our sense of joy should come from how we think and act within ourselves.

There is nothing wrong with trying to achieve wealth and power, but to the stoic, if it works out you should be happy, but you shouldn't depend on achieving that success to be happy. Otherwise your happiness will be inconsistent, taken away, or never achieved. Stoicism suggests that a successful person is someone who can be okay without the things he or she typically desires for comfort.

This doesn't mean stoics are people without emotion, though. They see human emotion as something that can be trumped by reason, because the position we take towards that emotion decides our mood. There's a quote from Marcus Aurelius that sums it up nicely - "Almost nothing material is needed for a happy life for he who has understood existence."

A stoic's ability to find happiness despite what occurs around them is developed through character and perspective. Nothing is good or bad inherently. Only our judgement and interpretations can be good or bad. A stoic strives for acceptance and indifference towards the events around them and focuses their attention on controlling their reactions.

The practice of stoicism is not easy, and it's impossible to be a perfect stoic that has no negative reactions or desires. However, stoicism gives us a target to strive for. As such, a common stoic practice is to stop oneself from indulging in the things that give them pleasure and comfort to prove to themselves how strong they are.

This practice is to prepare a stoic for situations where they will face physical hardships and to help train the stoic to not desire things outside their control. You can think of this like a dopamine fast but with a different ruleset. A dopamine fast is meant to starve you of anything that provides dopamine for 24 hours to reset and refresh your mind, but for the stoic practice, it is more lenient because it is meant to build character. As for the stoic exercise to deal with negativity, it is called negative visualization.

You simply imagine bad things that will happen to you. Marcus Aurelius used this daily when he had to confront people who weren't so nice to deal with. By starting the day with negative visualization, he was able to be mentally prepared to confront those people. You might think that negative visualization will make your day worse, but it can make your day better when you realize all these bad things you visualized didn't happen to you. Another exercise is memento mori, which is the stoic reminding themselves that life is temporary and short. This way, he or she won't waste time on trivial things.

Life is short, and that is why it is important to direct our energy towards the important things. Stoicism can help give us guidance in this chaotic world full of distractions by helping us find peace from within.

Stoicism Rules to Follow in the Modern Era

1. **Become Honest** - This can take you so far in your journey to become a successful modern stoic. Just be honest in whatever you do and whatever you say. Being honest can save a lot of your time and the time of others, too. Whether in a relationship, professional commitment, or any other connection, honesty is at the core of being a stoic in the modern day.

2. **Stay comfortable** - Some modern people are used to this already, but I have to emphasize this trait for everyone. Your dressing, living, and general behavior has to be in a flow of comfort. This is a way to remain in harmony with yourself and your life, allowing stoicism to come more easily.

3. **Make your way** - If the path is not obvious, make your way. This mindset can save you from facing failures and backlashes. Just by changing your attitude about how you see things can be the biggest step of your life. Time has changed, so you too have to change yourself.

4. **Be real** - In both your expectations and your promises, be realistic. Your real intentions and words can save your heart from getting broken. Being real is the biggest

key to modern stoicism and it can also be taught to children. They learn how to behave and what they can expect from others.

5. **Cut out ego from your life** - Ego can be your biggest enemy. You have to phase it out of your behavior to become contented and successful. An egoistic person can lose everything they care about. Thus, modern stoicism is all about being realistic and free from any negativity.

Stoicism can be applied to modern life quite effectively. But, there can also be some limitations to the stoic philosophy. For example, a stoic has to give up on some important things. By giving up on something, you may realize that your priorities will suffer. You may act oddly to your family and close friends.

When someone faces his or her fears, insecurities, and gives an analyzing shift to their thoughts, it can become difficult. As stoicism is not an easy practice, you may find it hard to cut down on your desires and to live a life on strict values.

The implementation period of stoicism can be really long. It may be difficult to change or adapt to new behaviors and habits. The amount of time it takes can vary from person to person, since we can't change ourselves in just a matter of a few days. You may also feel the urge to deviate back to your non-stoic life, but it is worth a try to become a stoic.

Being stoic is a cumbersome process. You may find it hard to stay committed to doing the meditations. But, make sure you are willing to read some books like this one and see if you can get your friends and family members to discuss stoicism with you.

If you find it difficult to adapt the methods and teachings of stoicism, find a mentor. Someone who has already applied these methods in their own life. Or, if you want to keep it private, read books and study the philosophy to add to your stoic knowledge.

Controlling emotions might be troublesome for you in some situations. The fact that it is troublesome may also bother you. You may find it a little draining psychologically while practicing stoic behavior. Don't lose hope. You can always mix and match the old and modern stoicism and see what works for you and what does not.

Chapter 9: How to Practice Stoicism with Practical Exercises

Let's get on to three stoic exercises that you can start applying today. The very first stoic exercises to train your perceptions is to avoid the good and the bad. Here's a quote from Marcus Aurelius that addresses this: "Choose not to be harmed and you won't feel harmed." Science has proven recently through behavioral therapy that Marcus Aurelius was right, and he was right some 2,000 years ago. He said that in life, events happen again and again. You have perceptions of these events, you have opinions of these events, and these perceptions and opinions of the events are what make you feel a certain way.

It is not the events that cause you to feel harm, it is your perception of those events that will cause you to feel harmed. For example, there may be two men waiting for a bus. Now, the bus is really late, so the same event is happening to both of these two men. But, one man's perception of the bus is different than the other man's perception. One man is annoyed at the bus because he is thinking that the bus is late and it's wasting his time. Because this perception of the event is negative, his emotions are negative. But the second man's perceptions of the event is different. He's thinking great, the bus is late, now I have more time to relax and think about life. Because they have two different perceptions about the event, they have two different emotions about the event. Therefore, it is not the event that causes you to feel a certain way. It is your perception, your opinions, and your judgments of an event that cause you to feel a certain way. So when a negative event happens to you, try and reframe it. Turn the obstacle around and look for the positive side of the obstacle that will cause you to feel a better way. Now, a very common way that you can do this is when someone or something is late. For example, you could train yourself to recognize that these are times for you to practice your values. You can now practice patience, and that is how you flip around any obstacle to make you feel better about whatever happens in your life.

It can be really valuable to your life when you start implementing it. If the bus is late, then great, you've got an opportunity to practice patience, and that's how you should view it in your mind. But you can use the same for any negative event that happens in your life. If someone is annoying you at work, great! Now you get to practice keeping your head cool. If someone breaks up with you, great, now you have time to improve yourself. Now you have time to go through the mental steps that it takes for you to overcome pain. Once you've done that, you'll come out better on the other side.

Every single negative event that happens in your mind can be reframed into a positive event. Another exercise that you can apply to get better results in your life is called a "view from above," or a "bird's eye view." This allows you to see everything all at once and take in the big picture.

This exercise encourages you to view yourself from a third-person point of view. Remove yourself from your emotions by pretending that you're looking at yourself outside of yourself. Detach yourself from your emotions, because when you are detached from your emotions you can look logically at decisions. You can recognize how small your problems are and you can recognize just how many people out there have the same problems as you. When you're worrying, when you're stressed, and when you're anxious about a problem, zoom out. Now, view the world from above, and recognize that first of all your problems are tiny in comparison to the grand scheme of life, and second, recognize how many other people in the world have similar or even worse problems than you. And how many people overcome that problem.

Then there is memento mori. What this means is you should meditate on your death. Here's what Seneca has to say - suppose you are going to die soon. The end is near. In this case, you know that you will never take any day for granted. What this means is that you should think about your death, be fully aware, and fully accustomed to the fact that you will die.

You could die today or you could die tomorrow or you could die in a week's time. As soon as you recognize that life is short and that it could end at any moment, you recognize the importance of every single second of your life. You see, the problem is that we all think that we have more time than we do. We take each day for granted and we waste time every single day. That is, until we meditate and focus on the fact that we could die at any second. You could get hit by a car tomorrow. Death is so easy. It's so close to us, and we spend our whole lives avoiding death even though it's just around the corner and could take us at any moment. So use that not to get depressed, but as an encouragement to live every single second of your life to the best of your potential, to the best that you ever can be. Because if you die tomorrow or today, you want to do so knowing you did everything you could to be everything you could be.

Here's an excellent quote about stoicism that sums it all up very nicely - "Objective judgment, now, at this very moment. Unselfish action, now, at this very moment. Willing acceptance, now, at this very moment." - Marcus Aurelius, Meditations IX.6

To live a tremendous life, these things are so important. Stoicism says that objective judgment, unselfish action, and willing acceptance are all that you need in life.

A calm mind can be a blessing in this messy and chaotic world. Some people have chosen abusive methods like pills and other substances which can lead to addiction. If you want to achieve inner peace in a healthy and non-medicated way, stoicism has some valuable methods to offer.

Stoic Exercises to Change Your Life

Negative Visualization

Optimism is a dark side when you reflect a belief or hope that your life or a specific aspect of it is going to be favorable and positive. You possibly set yourself up for disappointment. That's why so many people start their day with a positive attitude and get defeated by the harsh and ugly realities of life by the end. Stoics have a way to counter-attack life's ugliness using a technique called negative visualization.

Negative visualization actually takes strength from pessimism by mentally preparing you for undesirable and uncomfortable situations. Marcus Aurelius said the following regarding this: "Begin each day by telling yourself 'Today I shall be meeting with interference, ingratitude, insolence, disloyalty, ill-will, and selfishness.'" By visualizing the negativity combined with an accepting attitude, Marcus Aurelius managed his expectations and shielded his soul against adversity to achieve self-control.

Practicing the ability to control oneself can be very useful in order to stay away from addictive behavior and acting on your impulses when it's better not to, and to remain focused on the things that truly matter to you. Stoics make a clear distinction between the things we can control and the things we cannot control. Epictetus said that things which are in our control are: our opinions, pursuit, desire, and aversion. This directly points towards our actions. Things which are not in our control can be explained as whatever we can't control by our own actions. The key is strengthening the things in our control, which takes practice.

There are different ways to do this. An example is intermittent fasting, in which you don't eat for a specific amount of time. Another example is chewing your food a certain number of times before you swallow it. The last one seems easy, but when you're a glutton like me, when it comes to food it's actually very difficult.

The last method is to practice not giving up. After swallowing your food, or after chewing it for ten to twenty times, why don't you start eating like a pig? Don't use your hands and just go for it, especially in a restaurant so everyone can see what you're doing. This is a way to combat a trait that most of us have — caring too much about the opinions of other people.

The thing is, the opinions of other people are not up to you, so why worry about them? Because of our social conditioning, it takes practice to break this habit. A fear of social ostracism is deeply ingrained within us. By deliberately making a fool of ourselves, we will be exposed to situations in which people will judge us negatively even if it's just through looks or giggles. Slowly, you'll experience that this doesn't hurt as you've imagined. Thus, you don't give up and your attitude will become stronger.

Journaling

Journaling involves writing your thoughts down and is a practice done by stoics to find relief and create a sense of order in their thoughts and memories. Therefore, journaling has a very cathartic effect on the mind. Perhaps the most famous stoic who kept a journal is Marcus Aurelius. In fact, his journal can be read in book form and has been mentioned or quoted several times thus far. This work was never meant to be published, because it was a personal diary of Marcus. Epictetus and Seneca, both stoic philosophers, practiced some form of journaling as well. Seneca spoke about it in the following words: "When the light has been removed and my wife has fallen silent, aware of this habit that's now mine, I examine my entire day and go back over what I've done and said, hiding nothing from myself, passing nothing by."

Memento Mori

"Remember you must die." The practice of memento mori means reminding ourselves that we are going to die. Thinking about the reality of death puts your life in perspective and tells you that your life is ticking away second by second, and that we should not waste it on trivial things. Also, it teaches us to live life more fully because tomorrow we might as well be dead. Thinking about death should not evoke fear, but gratitude and appreciation for the life that has been given to us. Seneca said that we should be prepared for death. He said we should postpone nothing and live our lives to the fullest. Someone who lives as if it is their last day can never run out of life.

View From Above

Think about the fact that the Earth is a simple sphere zooming around in space. This sphere that is our home is just a small planet in our solar system and completely dwarfed by the bigger planets like Jupiter and Saturn, and let's not even take into account the Sun. The Sun itself is a small star compared to many other stars in our solar system, which is just one of the many many systems in the Milky Way. When we realize how small we are, it becomes much easier to let go of the many trivialities of our human existence.

That annoying co-worker, your mother-in-law, the guy who cut you off in traffic—none of these things are significant anymore. When we see them from a cosmic point of view, even larger events like wars, natural disasters, and other tragedies are minor events. If we realize how vast the universe is, we realize how small we are. It's humbling and it puts our existence in perspective. Once we arrive at this new perspective, occasionally it makes us giggle at people who are triggered and upset by stupid, meaningless things.

Now for the view from above exercise. Firstly, picture yourself in the same room outside of your body looking upon yourself. Now pay attention to yourself and everyone around you on the same floor of your house. Now picture everyone in your house, with yourself at the center. Now zoom out and picture everyone that's on your street. You'll picture everyone in your neighborhood. Zoom out again with you in the center and imagine everyone in your city, each with their own individual lives. Now imagine everyone in your country. Zoom all the way out as if you're looking at Google Maps. Imagine everyone's problems, and finally zoom out to where you're looking at Earth. Picture all the people in different countries, each with their own individual lives, each with their own problems, each with their own families. This exercise is a good way to help you overcome emotional hurdles and put things in perspective.

Amor Fati

When we worry, we are concerned with a certain outcome. We want the future to be such and such, and we dread the idea of things going completely the other way. Worrying about the future creates anxiety, and stoics have a very simple check for this called Amor Fati. The Latin phrase "amor fati" means "loving fate." Whatever happens in your life, as long as you embrace the outcome you'll be fine. This doesn't mean that we should become nihilistic and do nothing. Goals and ambitions are fine, as long as you remain detached from the outcome. Say you're a musician. You practice as hard as you can and write the best music possible, but you remain detached from the outcome. At the same time, your focus will shift from a concept and goal somewhere in the future to the present moment, which lightens you from worrying about undesirable outcomes. As a result, your work improves and you have a greater chance of success.

Constantly Examine Your Impressions

You might often be tempted to deliberately react to some situations or some conversations. This is due to human nature. But take a step back. Analyze everything and make room for some calculations. Avoid rash emotional reactions and ask yourself whether you should react to this situation, or if it is even under your control. If it is not under your control, leave it. If you have control over that situation, give a calculated reaction.

Detach Yourself From Unworthy Things

Your family, friends, and some close relations deserve your love. But if you are attached to insignificant or material things like a necklace, your favorite pair of shoes and so on, then you must stop. Save yourself from the misery that comes with valuing possessions. After all, everything you own is temporary.

Reserve Clause

Nothing is under your control, but you can control your thoughts and behavior. The reserve clause exercise gives you a trailer of future events. We should approach doing anything with the stoic reserve clause. Fate permits us, whenever planning an action, to mentally rehearse with this method. If you are heading out somewhere, picture yourself in that environment. Imagine people bustling around, yelling, possibly bumping into you or being rude. Just imagine everything in advance. Be prepared for your future. Remind yourself that you are prepared for any behavior that might be thrown at you.

The power of the mind can be easily seen if we look at examples of what happens within our thoughts when something happens to other people versus when that same thing happens to us. Naturally, it is far easier to maintain calm when an inconvenience or even disaster is happening to someone other than ourselves. We can use this to our advantage by applying the same detachment in our own situations as we do the situations of others.

An example of this would be when we see someone's car broken down on the side of the road. We may feel bad for them, maybe even stop to help, but we'll hardly be devastated. However, when that same event happens to us, we're frustrated, upset, angry, and all because it impacts us and our lives. Why should there be any difference, though? The situation is the same. Your reaction is what has changed.

To tie this back to the reserve clause, whenever you are thrown into a situation that you want to react negatively to, think about what you would do if it were happening to a stranger. Look at it from an outside perspective with no emotional attachment. Then react accordingly.

Talk Less

This one might be a little difficult for the professional speaker or talkative person. But this is the best habit one can acquire. Only talk when it is required, and instead listen more attentively. Also endeavor never to speak when you are upset or angry. When your emotions are in charge, your brain is not.

Choose Your Company

It is up to you and your own beliefs as far as how you choose to live your life. However, remember that your company is a reflection of you. Thus, make sure you spend your time with the right people. These people can include anyone, family or friends, as long as they are compatible with your view of the world. You should closely pay attention to whom you spend your time with and evaluate if their emotional intelligence level is a match with your own. If someone you associate with isn't a good person, how do you expect them to make your life better? Life is all about the decisions we make, and those decisions include the company we keep. Stoicism reminds us how important it is to value the right friendships and relationships.

Face Insults with Calmness

If someone insults you, try not to respond in kind. There is no reason to react emotionally, especially since it will not make the situation better. In most cases, an insult from someone says more about them than it does about you. If you respond with the same kind of venom, you will be on the same level as they are. Stoicism is about rising above, so treat insults with a calm detachment. They'll have less of an effect on you, and you won't compromise your own image or integrity.

Don't Speak Too Much About Yourself

Extroverts might find this difficult to practice, but trust me, it is remarkable. Don't overshare or brag about your experiences, possessions, qualities, adventures, etc. Other people are often just not that interested. Or, they'll feel like you're more interested in yourself than in them, and there is no better way to end a conversation. There should always be a give and take. Give a small amount of information, then listen attentively.

Speak Without Judging

To adopt this habit, you have to start speaking according to the facts. We generally speak about whatever is on our minds, and often we speak hastily. Hasty speaking means hasty judgement. Imagine how much better the world would be if we didn't judge, though. What if we looked at human affairs in a more matter-of-fact manner. If someone drinks a lot, don't call them a drunk. Simply observe that they like a glass of wine now and again. If a friend is often complaining, don't think of them as a downer. Observe that they speak about the events in their life that cause them pain. Unless they ask for your opinion, refrain from giving one, even in your own head. Are there any habits you have that you wouldn't want someone else judging? It's the same for everyone you encounter.

Life is Short, Make the Best of It

Human life is incredibly brief, especially when you take into consideration the timescale of the universe. We are a blip on the map, and yet we waste the little time we have feeling sad, hurt, angered, and focus on all the wrong things. We become obsessed with wealth, material possessions, and our reputations, none of which will matter once we're gone. Stoicism wants you to remember that. Remember how brief it all is, and add back that sense of wonder to your life. Marvel at the fact that you exist at all. When you realize that you're less than a grain of sand in this wide universe, you appreciate yourself and your life more.

Get Inspiration

A stoic will often seek someone who can act as a mentor. Set a role model for your life and try to adapt their behavior. A role model can be like your guardian angel who will guide you to a better way of life. This inspiration can be anyone, from a member of your family to a friend.

Discomfort

Don't be afraid to feel some discomfort every now and again. This could be in the form of sleeping on the floor, eating at a cheap restaurant, buying items from a dollar store instead of brand names, etc. Try this once or twice a month to remember how much you should appreciate the simple pleasures and small comforts that you're able to afford or have access to.

Sickness and Pain are Opportunities

Do you feel in pain while you are sick? Are you intolerant to the misery? This exercise can be good for you. Turn your pain into an opportunity and see how tolerant you become. According to stoicism, pain belongs to the body, not the mind. So, you can feel the pain through the body but not through the mind. For example, if you have a fever, take it as an opportunity to rest. In this way, you will no longer see pain as a hindrance.

Opportunity

Opportunity abounds in this world, but most of us are blind to it. We fill our minds with junk that blocks out the real experiences and the opportunities, then we complain that we can't move forward in life. I've experienced this, and it's pretty straightforward. Do you think about it the amount of energy you get back when you're not dissipating it all that? Be conscious that your unconscious mind isn't chewing on all that stuff from the nonsense pop culture TV, must watch shows, whatever to the news and the echo-chamber of fear that's created in the world. When you separate yourself at a healthy level and of course you choose to engage, you're a good citizen and a good participant in society. But you draw some bright line boundaries around it. You get so much energy back that's astonishing. And one of the things you may want to care a lot less about is the social comparison side of what other people are doing. Maybe a little less Twitter, a little less Instagram and a little more of what you're here to do would be a good idea.

Epictetus was an old-school, intense teacher. He was a former slave who then became freed and then he became a prominent stoic philosopher. So he had a school where a lot of the young kind of nobility came to training. He was a super intense guy. He was the greatest influence on Marcus Aurelius. What's interesting is that a Roman Emperor philosopher learned from a former Roman slave the philosophy that he practiced unbelievably diligently.

Then we have Seneca, the third stoic, who was the era's greatest playwright. He was a power broker one of the wealthiest people in Rome. Fascinating trio!

The three of them used metaphors around fighting, rustling, and boxing. These were their big metaphors, kind of like how we use basketball and football as metaphors for our lives today. Their sport of choice was something called pankration, which literally means all strength. It's kind of a more pure form of UFC, the mixed martial arts of today. Pankration, full strength. Epictetus would counsel his young nobleman and he would say, "Look, what kind of boxer are you if you're in the ring? You get hit in the face and then you just walk out of the ring." He said, "What kind of boxer are you if you aren't going to get hit?" That's the whole point of competing in that type of sport. It's an opportunity to show up with your full strength, and if you walk out of the ring that actually doesn't have any consequence. But if you get hit in life, which is inevitable, the same way you're going to get hit if you're in a boxing ring, and you walk out of life and you give up, then what kind of boxer are you?

He said that, most importantly, what are you training? For the whole point of your training is that if you're a boxer or a wrestler or whatever a human being is able to be, to deal with a really strong opponent is the whole point. You want the best opponent you can get. You want life to challenge you. You set big, aggressive, exciting goals that are challenging yet doable and meaningful. Knowing you're going to have challenges, and knowing it's going to force you to rise to your absolute best. So when you get hit and you're ready to walk out, thinking about it first. These philosophers' notes and the optimal living classes and all the other work is for you to optimize your life. It is all about being able to deal with life's challenges. You have to remember that this is why you train, that's what you want to say. When you face a challenge, rub your hands together and say "What's the tool and the weapon I need to bring to this battle right now?" Remember that this is about being a warrior of the mind, not a librarian. Be a good life boxer. Show up for opportunity and do your best.

Everything You Have is a Borrowed Item from the Future

Yes, you read that right. Everything can be taken from you in a second. The only thing you have that is truly yours is your mind. And even then, one day you will no longer have a body or mind. Everything from your toes to your phone is borrowed and won't be yours one day. Enjoy everything while you have it. It's all here for a limited time only.

Count Your Blessing

You must stay aware of your blessing. Your family, friends, all of these things are your blessings. You shouldn't ask for things you can't have, just focus on what you already have. On the other hand, you should also not get attached to the things you consider as your blessings. The point of blessings is that they're special and precious, and therefore deserve to be treated with love and respect, not possessiveness.

Don't Blame Someone Who Does Something Wrong to You

When someone does anything to you, it's right according to their perception. You shouldn't blame such a person. Instead, have pity or be kind to them, and don't consider taking revenge. Learn to move on.

Become Tranquil

This exercise is to practice calmness even in adverse situations. It will be worth practicing stoicism by including this exercise. If there is a situation which is making you angry, remind yourself that you have to choose tranquility instead. Seneca talks about a Greek word, "amia," which directly translates as tranquility. How we achieve a state of tranquility?

There are two ways - you need to have a sense of clarity, and you need to know who you are, what's important to you, and then you need to have the courage to live in that way. That's actually the essence of it. What can get in the way of this, however, is self-doubt and a lack of confidence or second guessing yourself. You can feel that something is a part of your path, who you are, and what you are meant to be doing, but then you second-guess that sense. When this happens, your tranquility is gone, you become anxious, and you begin comparing yourself to others.

You feel that you are not keeping up with other people around you or that you encounter. Instead of doing this, ignore what other people are doing and stop second guessing yourself. Stay on your path. Of course it will evolve, but have the confidence, the clarity, and the courage to step forward. That's the essence of tranquility. So think about who you are, what your gifts are, and how you are committed to giving them to the world. Commit to that every day. Do the work to find clarity and move forward.

Daily Lifestyle

Epictetus and Marcus Aurelius taught everyone how to live life through a stoic method. Stoicism permeates our culture in ways a lot of us aren't really familiar with. But often, we wonder where to start. Stoicism is the distinction between that which is within our control and that which is outside of our control. So, the whole practice of stoicism ultimately, or one aspect anyway, the central aspect, comes down to distinguishing between the things that are within our control and the things that are outside of our control.

The wise stoic philosopher is always doing the math, thinking *Is this within my control or not?* And guess what? The only things that are within our control are our thoughts, behaviors, and our response to what's happening in the world. So, we can't change our past, we can't predict with 100% certainty the future, and we can't do anything about what's happening right now. What we can do and what we can control is whether or not we choose to step forward with virtue. Whether we choose to do our best every day.

That's the essence of stoicism, and it's reflected in the serenity prayer. You can adapt the serenity prayer in your daily life and take the maximum benefits of stoicism. In this prayer, you have to ask God (or whatever higher power you believe in) to grant you the serenity to accept the things you can not change and courage to change the things that are under your control. This is the shortest but the strongest exercise in stoicism. You can do it anytime you feel worried, in danger, or in any difficult situation. The ancient philosophers weren't cataloging these ideas much. They weren't librarians of the mind like a lot of modern-day academic philosophers are. They were warriors of the mind they were striving to embody these ideas. No idea was more important than this: knowing what's within our control, knowing what is not, and then choosing to respond.

Acquiescence

Ancient stoics had a couple of practices like reserve clause that we already mentioned,, which basically means that before a stoic does anything, they think *Yes, I want to do this. This is my target, and I'll do it unless something else intervenes.* They always know that the outcome is not within their control, and they call that the reserve clause.

The second practice is what they call the art of acquiescence, or acquiesce to reality. They don't fight reality. If a storm arises while they're at sea, or they get hit in the face when they're in the boxing ring, they don't moan about it and think *Why is this happening to me?* They acquiesced to it. They roll with it, and although it was written about and found thousands of years ago, it is still an amazing practice of stoicism.

Stoics said not only should you accept what happens to you via acquiescence, you should also love it. You should love your fate, and act as if you wanted that to happen. Basically, act like you scripted this negative thing, so you can rise up to it.

Any time you try to get rid of something in your life, you also get rid of all of your power. So, the art of acquiescence is again remembering rule number one, which is that the only thing you have control over is your response to a situation. So you have to love what it is.

Think about anything in your life that you might be fighting, and think if you can look at the lesson in that. Use it to get a little bit stronger. That's what you have to become. Better and better. Rub your hands together with challenges rather than run out of the ring. Train yourself to say yes and accept whatever life throws your way.

Ignore the Opinions of Others

There are some important sayings which Marcus said about other people's opinions. Why do we care so much about other people's opinions? We are social creatures, and many of us learn from an early age that we need to fit in. We don't want to be labeled as weird or different, so we conform and try to fit in with everyone else. This behavior starts right from childhood. Children often develop a self-image that is reliant on others. Such people live according to the opinions of others, and this impacts their whole life. They seek approval and some sort of validation from others in the form of praise and approval. This validation tends to make us worried about whether this image is correct or not. So, you're constantly asking for validation from friends, family, colleagues and even complete strangers. Sadly, many of us buy things we don't need with money we don't have to influence strangers or someone whom we don't even like.

This can be easily understood by the Looking-Glass Self Concept. According to this concept, firstly we create an image of how others see us, then we create a judgment of that appearance, and then we create our own self-concept through the judgment of others. We then perceive this judgment to be either favorable or unfavorable. It is utterly wrong to perceive ourselves according to another person's point of view or to see ourselves as another person's opinion. You can't control someone else's opinion, so this is a game that can't be won.

I'll say it again: constantly trying to validate yourself according to others is a doomed practice. You're basically handing over your self-worth to someone else. People's opinions oftentimes have nothing to do with you at all. So why give them this power? No one should have that kind of control over you except yourself. In this way, you are becoming their prisoner.

So, with all that said, this is what Marcus stated about the opinions of others: he said that you should not waste your life for the sake of thoughts of others. A person should be willing to take opinions only from their loved ones. Marcus stressed that everyone can be wrong at some point in their life, so don't worry about what others say, let alone their opinions. He even advised not to take praise from such people. When someone is not satisfied with themselves, how can they praise you with utter honesty? You can still be friends with them, but don't count on their words. Marcus also reaffirmed that everything is in your power. How you take that opinion is what matters the most. You should not please everyone, as this is not your duty. However, Marcus even mentioned that you should also be aware of your own opinions. So, it's obvious that we should try our best to stop giving so much value to others' opinions. You simply don't need them. Look within instead.

Here are a couple more reasons why you should cast away others' opinions: when you're living your life based on others' opinions of you, you're giving up your own authentic inner voice, you're not being your true self, and you're not living up to your potential. You won't be happy living a life dictated by other people. The people who live by their inner voices are leaders. Those that don't are followers, and followers are never the first to do something of importance. You'll be more respected for being your own person and upholding your values, opinions, and morals.

Always say whatever is the truth. Someone who says the truth or who lives by their own terms can live peacefully on their own. You can respect yourself and be confident when you live in such a way, and other people will be respectful towards you. If you have a dream, fulfill it. No one else can stand in your shoes. Think about your purpose rather than what others think. Your own intellect or your inner voice can guide you to achieve what others have not. Such people may face objections and badmouthing. But every great man has faced his own set of challenges. They don't know what they're talking about all the time but they still do it, and they change the world.

Need some examples of outcasts and people who stood up for their beliefs even when everyone was against them? Just look at Galileo, Joan of Arc, Martin Luther, Robert Oppenheimer, Vincent Van Gogh, and Edgar Allan Poe.

Empower your true self. Remember that you can do anything. People will always judge you, and there isn't a single thing you can do about it, so do what you want anyway. Most people don't care what you're doing. They don't care because they're too wrapped up in their own drama. They're probably too worried thinking about what people think of them. Do you want proof? What's the first thing you look at when you look at a group photo? Probably yourself. People in social situations are the same exact way. They're focusing on themselves, not you.

Change Any Situation

How can you get a stoic mindset shift that you can implement straightaway? When you have a negative situation, it's very easy to flip that negative situation and make it positive. I'll start off with a quote from Epictetus: "Men are disturbed not by things, but by the view which they take of them." When something bad happens to you or a negative situation occurs, instead of dwelling on how negative it is, how bad it is, and how it makes you feel, think of it as an opportunity for you to practice one of the virtues.

So picture this: you've got a really bad cold or you're ill and you're just lying in bed. You can't go to work. Instead of contemplating and dwelling on how bad this makes you feel that there's nothing you can do, and that you're missing work, use it as an opportunity to do something productive for your life, like contemplate your existence, or meditating, or whatever it may be. All negative things that happen in life are just a chance for you to practice a virtue.

Control your life

Stoicism teaches us about being in control of our lives, not being victims, and taking extreme ownership of everything that happens to us. I believe that there's one other topic that goes hand-in-hand with that concept. But I believe that a lot of people are depressed because of these two things combined: first of all, they feel out of control and second of all, their perspective of life is out of whack. It's off and it's not correct because perspective is this amazing thing that completely changes how you view the world.

Happiness equals reality over expectations. This means that your happiness will increase as your reality gets better. I agree with this, and your actual reality will increase as your expectations get smaller. So if you can reduce your expectations of what's happening in your life, then you can become happier.

Now, the stoic ancient philosophers 2,000 years ago agreed with this. They had this idea of negative visualization that when you expect something negative to happen or at least expect something worse than what actually will happen, then that's better for you. Then, if that thing actually happens, you're prepared for it. And if something better than that thing that you're expecting to happen happens, then you're happier. Now, it's a minor thing that can be applied to your own life. Suppose you are about to move into a new flat or maybe new student accommodations. You are in your second year of college, and as you are moving into your room you do a little bit of negative visualization.

Imagine that your room will be horrible, tiny, and grim. When you move into this new room, you will be happy no matter what it will be like. Because obviously, student accommodation flats aren't that good. We all know that, but because you had negatively visualized what your room is going to be like, your expectations will be minimized so your happiness will end up increasing. This whole idea of perspective and shifting your perspective is such a powerful tool. You can also use it to become fulfilled when you face depression. And if you recognize how lucky you are, you are not depressed in a situation where someone else might be. It will increase your happiness. This should not be perceived as an offense to someone who is depressed. If you have depression, then you can look up to someone who can't walk or stand. This is what stoicism is in a nutshell. How can you be depressed when you recognize how lucky you are?

Obviously, there are people with the chemical imbalances but for the people that don't have that genetic disposition, how can you be depressed when you've recognized how lucky you are? We live better than Kings lived years ago. We have many facilities that were lacking in the past. We are so lucky, and we're lucky because we're human. Think of all the different species you could have been. You could have been a camel. Even if you were the best camel in the world, even then you would not have as good as life as you have as a human. It's true! The best anything or the happiest something isn't as happy as you could be and isn't as lucky as you are. The fact that you're human and you're able to read this book is amazing. How lucky you are! Again, shift your perspective, recognize how lucky you are, and let gratitude flow through your body. If you want to be grateful, you've got to focus on the things that you're grateful for, because then you get to focus on only what you want to focus on, which should be being grateful. Take out five minutes a day and spend that time focusing on the things that you're grateful for. Don't just think logically about what you're grateful for, keep scanning your mind until you find something that triggers a feeling deep in your gut. Only then will you get to know what are you truly grateful for.

You Don't Feel Afraid of Death

Let us balance life's perks each day. You should count each day and analyze every second. Live each day as if it may be your last one. Everyone repeats it, but only a few people understand what it actually means. No, it does not mean that you should inject heroin because you're going to die anyway, and no it does not mean you should throw all morals out the window because the world is going to end. You should picture it just like this - you're a soldier leaving for deployment tomorrow. The day prior, you handle your business. You tie up any loose ends, you don't waste time arguing, you remind your loved ones that you love them and you're fully present. During the last few hours, you'll spend them with your family. The morning before you leave you're completely ready to go. You hope you will come back alive but you're fully aware there's a possibility that you will not. Live every single day starting with the day just like this. If you think of this method and utilize it every day in your meditation, then you will live a stoic life.

The connection between stoicism and death can be easily identified. Marcus said you can die anytime and anywhere. This knowledge can be a perfect exercise to calculate your words and actions. Every day as I start my meditation, I tell myself this quote, as it's the best quote for me. It grounds me into the present moment and the point of it. For me it speaks of urgency, appreciation, and humility.

It doesn't matter if you're rich or poor, blonde or brunette, whether you have lots of work to do or if you're on vacation. Whatever the case seems to be, a truck could still crash into you and you could still die. And this could happen anytime, such as tomorrow or even today. Take a few minutes to appreciate how short your life actually is in the grand scheme of things. Remember that the world still spins whether you were there or not. Too many people realize how precious life is when it's far too late. This is why Marcus Aurelius reminded himself more than five times in his personal diary about how short life actually is. By contemplating mortality, it will help you focus on what's important and it will help you realize how small your problems are and how much time you waste being someone you don't want to be.

Bonus Meditation

By doing this meditation, you will be able to respond quite effectively in any situation. You will become the leader of your own life. First, prepare yourself for this meditation. Start by making yourself comfortable as much as you can. Lay on a bed, a carpet, a reclining chair, or simply your seat on the train. Cover yourself with something to keep you warm and lay back in a comfortable position with your legs slightly apart and the palms of your hands facing upwards. You are going to practice deep relaxation for about half an hour and when you end this meditation, you will awaken feeling renewed and empowered.

Begin to take three deep breaths in order to begin the relaxation process. Inhale deeply filling your whole body with a sense of warmth and relaxation. Exhale as you release any tension in your face, your shoulders, and your whole physical body. Again, inhale deeply, filling your whole body with a sense of warmth and relaxation. Exhale as you release any tension and again inhale deeply, filling your body with warmth and relaxation. Exhale as you release any tension in your physical body.

Notice how relaxed you are feeling now, and as you are relaxing even deeper you will begin to notice your body feels as if it is sinking, as if it is so heavy that it is sinking into the chair or mattress. Next, you have to do a rotation of consciousness throughout your whole body. I will mention a few parts of your body and you will move your attention there, imagining a warm golden light in that area.

Let's begin with your head. Imagine a golden light all around your head. Now move this golden light to your forehead, your right eye, left eye, the right cheek, left cheek, and the lips. Now relax your jaw muscles. Relax your right shoulder and your left shoulder. Bring the golden light now to the abdomen area, the genital area, the whole right leg, the whole left leg and now bring your attention to your breathing.

As you inhale your abdomen rises. It inflates like a balloon, and as you exhale your abdomen falls. Notice this relaxing rise and fall. Now start counting your breaths backward from 12 to 0 as follows. I am inhaling 12, I am exhaling 12, I am inhaling 11, I am exhaling 11, and so on. Continue to count your breaths backward until zero.

When you reach the end, it's the time to bring to mind between five to ten things that made you grateful, joyful, and happy within the last 24 hours. If you can't think of enough incidents in the last 24 hours, expand to the last three days or the last week or last month. Think about these things that happen at work, things that happened when you were traveling, or in your free time. Pleasant and positive things that happen with your family or with your loved ones. It could be something big or it may be something small like a nice warm cup of hot tea. Express gratitude and bring back to mind the feeling of joy and the emotions you felt when these incidents occurred.

Take a few minutes to go through as many incidents of gratitude as you can think of, and as you imagine and bring back to mind these incidents and moments, make them as vivid as you can by incorporating all five senses. What will you hear, what will you taste, what or who will you touch, what will you smell, and picture the images. Make them as colorful and vivid as possible, and most importantly incorporate to the best of your ability the feeling of joy and happiness throughout your mind and body. Feel that feeling of gratitude from the top of your head to the bottom of your toes and know that when you express gratitude for beautiful moments in this life, you open the way for these moments to repeat themselves and to grow in terms of their magnitude.

Now we move on to release any negative charges. A negative charge is any feeling you might have towards a person or an incident towards which you might be harboring anger, resentment, jealousy, or any other toxicity. It could be a waiter who didn't treat you properly, a coworker who you had a disagreement with, a family member, or anyone else. It could be big or small, something that irritated you or something that is chronic and long-term. You will now mentally imagine that you are apologizing for any wrong that you brought to this person and see them apologizing back to you. On a deeper level we are all one, all connected, and any negative charge towards another living person or creature is in a way a charge against yourself. That's why we must rid ourselves of these negative charges or these toxic emotions.

When you finish expressing forgiveness to this person, see themselves forgiving you and you forgiving them. Imagine forgiveness moving from your heart outwards and then back towards your heart, and feel the calm and peace that engulfs your whole being. Of course, you need to note that when you're first starting out practicing this forgiveness exercise, you do it with situations where forgiveness is easier. Work your way upwards towards releasing more challenging feelings. Repeat this exercise with as many people with whom you have a negative charge. Simply repeat to yourself the phrases in your mind - "This thought is just an illusion, it really means nothing to me. I am free inside and nothing can harm me on the inside." Continue with "This thought is just an illusion. I can see the bigger picture of my life. I am free inside."

Chapter 10: Correlation between Stoicism and Buddhism

Some historians have said that stoicism was derived from Buddhism. Buddhists even came West and taught during the Roman Empire, and the Stoics were the result. I agree that Buddhism and Stoicism have similarities. Both are directed towards achieving and maintaining a mental state that we call equanimity. The word equanimity is perhaps a better word to describe this sense of detachment that the stoics are looking for than the words indifference. The mind state that the Buddhists want to achieve is called nirvana, which is similar to a mind state in stoicism. Because both point to peace of mind, being free of worry and rumination, Buddhist and stoic ways of dealing with external things or disturbers are quite similar. The Stoics use rational thinking to determine what things are up to us and what things are not up to us, and then decide that we shouldn't worry about the things that are not in our control.

The Stoics try to transcend what we call a value judgment, saying that we aren't harmed by the situation itself but by our judgments about that situation. An example: someone yells at you or insults you. What aspect of this event hurts you? The insult, or the way you process the insult? According to stoicism, it's the latter, and thus we can choose to feel offended or choose not to feel offended. In other words, we experience someone insulting us, then we judge the event and attribute a value to it. For example, an insult can be experienced as hostile, and we have the urge to punch that person in the face. Then, we make a conscious decision to do it. Instead, you can experience it not as hostile but as someone else's expression of dissatisfaction, and choose not to let it affect you. You decide that the reaction you could have is not beneficial to you, so you let it go.

Buddhists have a similar approach. The Buddha said that we have a choice to receive or reject an insult. One day, when a man angrily insulted the Buddha, he asked the man if you buy something for a person and he doesn't like it or want it, to whom does that gift belong? The man answered typically by saying "I will keep that present myself." To this Buddha said, "Right, this insult belongs to you because I don't want it, then the anger returns to you and you are the one who becomes sad, not me. All you have done is hurt yourself." So Buddhists as well as stoics are aware that we can choose to be disturbed by something. Both Stoicism and Buddhism are geared towards acceptance and not desiring things to happen, otherwise than they will happen.

Buddhists say that everything is impermanent. So, whatever will happen will cease to exist anyway. We don't have problems outside ourselves, it's just what the mind makes of it. We can't control the future, so why worry about it? Stoics have a concept called Amor Fati which is the love of fate, as we have discussed. This means that we should embrace whatever happens. This doesn't mean that we shouldn't strive for anything. We should actually strive for things that are virtuous. But we shouldn't be attached to the outcome. Attaching to the outcome will create worry, and worry is detrimental to our health. The Stoics and Buddhists agree that the best thing we can do is to live in the present moment. When we live in the present moment, we don't ruminate about the past and don't worry about the future. The present moment is all we have. Furthermore, it's the place where the future is made.

So the first similarity in both of these philosophies has to do with the goal. Both in stoicism and in early Buddhism there's a sense that we want to bring ourselves to a state of equanimity under all circumstances. We find that in both traditions. Now of course, in Buddhism there is more to the goal than that, particularly in traditional Buddhism.

The second similarity has to do with the method of reaching equanimity. We get ourselves to this position of equanimity through a long process of eliminating harmful greed, desire, hatred, anger, and ignorance. In both traditions, this is the case. Both traditions see greed as a problem, both traditions see anger hatred as a problem, and both traditions see ignorance as the deepest problem.

The third similarity has to do with their orientation of the philosophy in that it is practice oriented. It's not just about book learning. In some kinds of philosophies, the whole point of the philosophy is to know certain facts. This is not the case in either stoicism or Buddhism. The point is more about practice than it is about knowledge. Of course, knowledge is critical and crucial. In Buddhism you have right view, and in stoicism you have all kinds of knowledge about the world. But in both cases, what is really important is to use the philosophies as the practice.

The fourth similarity is their ethical focus. Both of them see the real point of the philosophy as one of ethics and of finding the best sort of life to live. This was what ethics meant in ancient Greece as well in ancient India. The point is to act in ways that are kind to other people and kind to yourself. That is going to get you the best sort of life. In a broad understanding of what that might mean, this has to do with what we can actually change. We can't change a lot of things, but we can certainly change our own ethical approach to behavior, to speech, and so on.

The fifth similarity between ancient Buddhism and stoicism is that they're both pragmatic philosophies. Both of them are philosophical. Some people were involved with creating these systems and elaborating on them. In essence, philosophers were interested in the theoretical aspects, but in neither case was it supposed to be philosophy. This was not simply an idle kind of way of thinking. Instead, it was supposed to be a practical philosophy. A pragmatic philosophy. We did things because they worked. The philosophical system was arrived at because the people arriving at that philosophy believed that it was the most skillful way of approaching reality.

Conclusion

I am so happy that you chose this book as your guide on your way to becoming a stoic. This book covered the practical aspects of the topic. The exercises can be a serious step towards your goal. This philosophy makes you a better human being. You learn how to deal with various situations. In turn, your life gets better with stoicism. Stoicism helps you to be able to carry yourself in a better way, whether it is emotionally or mentally. The more real you become by adapting stoicism, the easier it becomes for you to create a life that others dream about.

Don't forget to continue your stoic education beyond this book. Read the works of the great philosophers, discover their wisdom for yourself, and immerse your mind in the virtues and teachings of brilliant minds who came before. Many others have been on this journey before you. It would be wise to take a page from their book (perhaps literally) and see how you can apply stoicism in your everyday life. It is only with constant practice that we get better at anything, including philosophy.

I hope you had a great time reading about stoicism. This is a philosophy, but this is indeed a practical philosophy. Kings and emperors have utilized it, and now you can, too!

--

If you enjoyed this book and you want to go deep on Self Confidence and Self Discipline, please check my other books browsing "Charlie Holl" on Amazon.com. Thank you!

Bibliography

Encyclopædia Britannica. (February 03, 2019). Stoicism. Retrieved from https://www.britannica.com/topic/Stoicism

Internet Encyclopedia of Philosophy. (n.d). Retrieved from https://www.iep.utm.edu/stoicism/

Marcus Aurelius, Hard, R., Marcus Aurelius, & Fronto, M. (2011). Meditations. Oxford [England]: Oxford University Press.

Stoicism - By Branch / Doctrine - The Basics of Philosophy. (n.d). Stoicism. Retrieved from https://www.philosophybasics.com/branch_stoicism.html

Wikipedia. (July 04, 2019). Stoicism. Retrieved from https://en.wikipedia.org/wiki/Stoicism

9 781801 687713